# Recipes from a Pacific Northwest Inn

# Recipes
## from a
# Pacific Northwest Inn

❧

## Patti Swanson

ILLUSTRATIONS BY DALE INGRID SWENSSON

**Country Roads Press**
CASTINE · MAINE

Recipes from a Pacific Northwest Inn
© 1995 by Patti Swanson. All rights reserved.

Published by Country Roads Press
P.O. Box 286, Lower Main Street
Castine, Maine 04421

Text and cover design by Amy Fischer, Camden, Maine.
Illustrations by Dale Ingrid Swensson, Mt. Desert, Maine.
Typesetting by Typeworks, Belfast, Maine.

ISBN 1-56626-086-8


Library of Congress Cataloging-in-Publication Data

Swanson, Patti.
    Recipes from a Pacific Northwest inn / author, Patti Swanson ;
illustrator, Dale Swensson.
      p.    cm.
    Includes index.
    ISBN 1-56626-086-8  :  $12.95
    1. Cookery, American—Pacific Northwest style.    I. Title.
TX715.2.P32S93   1995
641.59795—dc20                                              94-38074
                                                            CIP

For information about the Inn, write or call:
Cashmere Country Inn
5801 Pioneer Drive
Cashmere, WA 98815

509-782-4212

*To my beloved husband, Dale, whose patience, support, and taste buds are never failing. My better half, you've enriched my life.*
*And to Julie, our ever-faithful employee and my right hand,*
*and our friends, family, and Cashmere Country Inn guests who have tasted, rated, and cheered me on throughout the years.*

*My heartfelt thanks.*

*Thou art great and Thou art good,*
*And we thank Thee for this food;*
*By Thy hand will we be fed,*
*Give us, dear Lord, our daily bread.*

—A child's prayer

# CONTENTS

# NTRODUCTION

I have a confession to make. I'm not an innkeeper because I fell in love with a beautiful 1907 farmhouse in the charming little town of Cashmere, Washington. Nor am I an innkeeper because of the fascinating and enjoyable people I meet from all over the world. Escaping the hustle and bustle of the city wasn't as big a motivation as people would like to think. The four beautiful and distinct seasons may have factored in somewhere—but none of these was the driving force behind the Cashmere Country Inn.

It was my love of food.

I have had a lifelong love affair with food. My parents were in the restaurant business. Some of my earliest and fondest memories are of standing in the restaurant kitchen watching the chef, Emil, sauteing, flambeing, and stirring sauces. That was enough to instill in me an endless fascination for food. To me, a fabulous meal is nothing short of magic.

In reviewing my career options, my choices naturally seemed to all center around cooking. When we lived in Seattle, my husband, Dale, and I would entertain often, but because that wasn't quite enough to satisfy my love of cooking, I began a small part-time catering business. During our travels we'd often stay at bed and breakfasts. Innkeeping kept coming into focus as the perfect way for me to do what I loved best: invite people to my home, entertain them, and—best of all—cook for them.

For years Dale and I pondered, scouted out different locations, and made lists of what we liked and didn't like about certain inns. When our delightful farmhouse came on the market, we jumped at the chance to buy it, and I found a way to turn my passion into a full-time job.

Becoming an innkeeper was the best thing that ever happened to me. When we served our first breakfast for an inn full of guests, I knew I had found my definition of heaven.

Six years later I still feel the same. There's nothing I enjoy more than cooking for our guests. Breakfast is my favorite meal, and the one I fix most often, but picnic lunches and dinners pose a pleasant challenge. It's always stimulating to try to find new and creative ways to surprise and delight our guests.

I feel especially blessed to live in Washington state, where there's a keen interest in what's fresh, new, and exciting on the culinary scene. I'm always in line to see what will be offered each season. Here in Eastern Washington, fresh fruit and produce are our forte. Our valley has an abundance of apples, and hazelnut trees grow in profusion. There are peach, pear, and cherry orchards as far as the eye can see. Ellensburg, famous for its lamb, is only an hour's drive, and the many nearby rivers boast trout and salmon. The surrounding mountains are a mushroom lover's dream; you'll often see fresh chanterelles offered for sale at the fruit stands along the highway.

Owning and operating Cashmere Country Inn for the last six years has truly been a labor of love for Dale and me, and we've met many unique and wonderful people. We've forged friendships that we treasure, and memories that will stay with us long after we've retired from innkeeping.

When Dale is serving dinner to guests poolside or in our dining room, he often says to me while I'm cooking, "I'd love to have this meal," or "I wish *we* could eat a meal like this—in a place like this." It makes me feel we've truly made it. What we're offering our guests is the hospitality, atmosphere, and delicious food that we ourselves would choose, given the opportunity. Who could ask for a better job?

If you've stayed with us before, we hope you enjoyed it as much as we enjoyed having you as our guest. If you've not had the chance to visit us, we'd like to extend a warm welcome. Our doors are always open, and my kitchen is warm and inviting. As George Bernard Shaw so aptly stated, "There is no love sincerer than the love of food." To that, I say a hearty "amen."

# EFORE YOU BEGIN

Over the years I've developed some basic cooking strategies that aid me in the kitchen. I'll pass them on. Pick and choose what works for you.

1. With a well-stocked kitchen, you can cook just about anything. See my list on what defines a well-stocked pantry.

2. When you're cooking, wear a loud, floral print apron. That way, the stains won't show.

3. Don't use inexpensive cookware.

4. Make sure you have an ample supply of wooden spoons, whisks, and spatulas.

5. Make your food attractive. The use of color and contrast in texture and shape makes even the simplest fare pleasing to the eye and stimulating to the appetite.

6. Don't let cooking intimidate you! Anyone can cook. Remember, Martha Stewart's first dinner party came straight out of Julia Child's cookbook. Chefs spend a considerable part of their lives studying the culinary arts; you don't need to compete with them. Just become familiar enough with cooking terms to read and understand recipes.

7. Read a recipe all the way through before you tackle it. Have handy all the ingredients listed, so they'll be at your fingertips when the recipe calls for them.

8. Don't ever use a damp towel or potholder for picking up hot pans. Moisture is a conductor of heat, and you'll burn yourself!

9. Make sure you season a dish more heavily if you'll be serving it cold. Chilling diminishes whatever fragrance or flavor is released by heating food. So if you've seasoned food when it's at room temperature, taste it again after it's cold; you may have to season it a bit more.

10. Don't ever cook with wine you wouldn't drink.

# THE WELL-STOCKED PANTRY

My philosophy is that in order to cook well, you must begin with a fully equipped kitchen. This doesn't mean you must have state-of-the-art equipment. It only means that you should have a good supply of staples and seasonings in your cabinets. That way you'll be prepared for anything from an impromptu supper for unexpected guests to an all-out "knock 'em dead" dinner.

## STAPLES

baking powder
baking soda
butter or margarine
catsup
cheese (Cheddar and Swiss)
chocolate (cocoa and baking chocolate)
coffee
cornmeal
cornstarch
dried red and navy beans
eggs
evaporated milk
flour (all-purpose)
garlic
gelatin (unflavored)
ginger (fresh)
herbs (fresh, in season, especially basil and mint)
lemons (fresh)
maple syrup
mayonnaise
milk
molasses
mustard (yellow and Dijon)
oil (olive and vegetable)
Parmesan or Romano cheese (not packaged "fresh pregrated")
pasta (dried)
potatoes
rice
salsa
sour cream or creme fraiche
stock (chicken and beef)
sugar (brown, granulated, and confectioners')
Tabasco Sauce
tomato sauce
tomatoes (canned)
vanilla and almond extracts
vegetable shortening
vinegar (cider, distilled white, red and white wine, and rice wine)
Worcestershire sauce
yeast
yogurt (plain)

## DRIED HERBS AND SPICES

allspice

basil

bay leaves

cayenne pepper

chili powder

cinnamon

cloves

cumin

curry

dill weed

garlic salt

ginger (ground)

mustard (dry)

nutmeg (whole and ground)

oregano

paprika

peppercorns (white and black)

rosemary

sage

salt

tarragon

thyme

# FOOD WEIGHTS AND MEASUREMENTS

Here are some standard measurements for reference if you need them. I find a chart like this helpful when I'm catering large parties and need to triple or quadruple a recipe. The opposite is true also; I use it just as much for cutting down recipes.

| | | |
|---|---|---|
| dash | = | less than ⅛ teaspoon |
| 3 teaspoons | = | 1 tablespoon |
| 1 tablespoon | = | ½ fluid ounce |
| 2 tablespoons | = | ⅛ cup (1 fluid ounce) |
| 4 tablespoons | = | ¼ cup (2 fluid ounces) |
| 5⅓ tablespoons | = | ⅓ cup |
| 8 tablespoons | = | ½ cup (4 fluid ounces) |
| 12 tablespoons | = | ¾ cup (6 fluid ounces) |
| 16 tablespoons | = | 1 cup (8 fluid ounces) |
| 1 cup | = | ½ pint (8 fluid ounces) |
| 2 cups | = | 1 pint (16 fluid ounces) |
| 4 cups | = | 1 quart (32 fluid ounces) |
| 2 pints | = | 1 quart |
| 2 quarts | = | ½ gallon |
| 4 quarts | = | 1 gallon |
| 16 ounces (dry) | = | 1 pound |

# Breakfast
# and
# Brunch

❖

# AMISH BAKED OATMEAL

SERVES 4

2 cups old-fashioned rolled oats
1½ teaspoons baking powder
½ teaspoon salt
1 cup milk
2 eggs, beaten
1½ teaspoons ground cinnamon

1 teaspoon vanilla extract
¼ cup vegetable oil
½ cup packed brown sugar
Vanilla yogurt, sliced fresh fruit, walnuts,
    and raisins, for accompaniment
Half-and-half, for accompaniment

Butter a 1-quart baking dish and set aside. In a large bowl combine the rolled oats, baking powder, and salt; set aside. In the container of a blender or in a small bowl, combine the milk, eggs, cinnamon, vanilla, oil, and brown sugar.

Pour the milk mixture into the oats mixture and stir to combine. Set aside for 5 minutes, stirring occasionally, then pour the mixture into the prepared baking dish and bake until set and golden (40 to 45 minutes). Serve with the yogurt, fruit, nuts, raisins, and half-and-half.

# $\mathcal{H}$EARTY ORCHARD GRANOLA

MAKES ABOUT 9 CUPS

4½ cups old-fashioned rolled oats (not quick cooking)
½ cup bran cereal
½ cup honey
¼ cup packed brown sugar
1½ teaspoons vanilla extract
1 teaspoon ground cinnamon
⅔ cup corn oil

⅓ cup orange juice
¼ teaspoon salt
½ cup chopped hazelnuts
¼ cup sesame seeds
½ cup sunflower seeds
½ cup raisins
1 cup ribbon coconut (*see Note*)
1 cup diced dried apples

Preheat the oven to 300°F. In a large bowl combine the rolled oats, bran, honey, brown sugar, vanilla, cinnamon, corn oil, orange juice, salt, hazelnuts, sesame seeds, and sunflower seeds. Blend well.

Spread the mixture on a greased baking sheet and bake until lightly browned (40 to 45 minutes), stirring every 10 to 12 minutes to prevent scorching. Stir in the raisins, coconut, and dried apples; let cool. Store any leftovers in an airtight container.

*Note:* Ribbon coconut is thickly sliced; you can find it in health food stores.

# BEULAH'S HOT DEVILED EGGS

SERVES 3

6 hard-cooked eggs, peeled
½ cup grated Swiss cheese

2 tablespoons chopped parsley

FILLING

2 tablespoons butter, melted
¼ teaspoon Worcestershire sauce
⅛ teaspoon garlic powder

¼ teaspoon minced parsley
2 teaspoons mild prepared mustard

SAUCE

2 tablespoons butter
2 tablespoons flour
1 cube chicken bouillon

1 cup milk
¼ teaspoon ground black pepper
½ teaspoon dry mustard

Preheat the oven to 350°F. Prepare the Filling and Sauce and set aside.

Slice the eggs in half; place the whites in a baking dish and the yolks in a medium bowl. To the yolks add the Filling and mix well. Transfer the yolk mixture to the baking dish with the halved egg whites.

Pour the Sauce over the egg mixture in the baking dish. Sprinkle with the cheese and bake until the cheese is melted (about 5 minutes). Sprinkle with the parsley.

*Filling:* Combine all the ingredients and mix well.

*Sauce:* In a small saucepan over medium-low heat, melt the butter. Add the flour and blend well. Crush the bouillon cube into the milk, then slowly whisk this mixture into the butter mixture, being careful to remove any lumps. Add the ground pepper and mustard and mix well.

> *Who can help love the land [France] that has taught us six hundred and eighty-five ways to dress eggs?*
> —Thomas Moore (1779–1852)

# BAKED EGGS IN A SOUR CREAM NEST

### SERVES 4

This is my most requested breakfast recipe. It's very simple, and can be multiplied or divided to fit any number. If you don't have individual ramekins, you can use custard cups or small souffle dishes. Or you can use a large casserole dish and divide the eggs at serving time.

2 tablespoons butter
¼ cup finely chopped onion
1 cup sliced mushrooms
½ cup cubed ham or smoked sausage
¾ cup sour cream
¼ teaspoon ground black pepper

2 teaspoons minced fresh dill or 1 teaspoon dried dill weed
8 eggs
4 tablespoons freshly grated Parmesan cheese

Preheat the oven to 500°F. In a large skillet over medium heat, melt the butter. Add the onion, mushrooms, and ham; saute until the onion is limp. Divide the mushroom mixture evenly among 4 greased ramekins or small casserole dishes.

In a small bowl combine the sour cream, ground pepper, and dill. Divide the mixture evenly among the ramekins, then smooth it in a circle to create a depression in the middle of each dish. Break 2 eggs into each depression, making sure that the eggs do not touch the edges of the dish (or they will cook unevenly). Top each with 1 tablespoon of the grated cheese. Bake until the eggs are set (7 to 10 minutes).

# ℰNCHANTMENT EGGS

### SERVES 6

Among the many pleasures of living in this valley is the accessibility to the Alpine Lakes Wilderness. The Enchantments are a series of beautiful little lakes nestled in the mountains not far from here. One morning my husband, Dale, was busy planning a trip there, and his whole topic of conversation was the Enchantments. I was cooking this egg dish, which in the past had been without a name. When he asked what I was serving the guests for breakfast, I responded, ''Enchantment Eggs!'' For better or worse, the name has stuck. This is a wonderful dish to serve when company's coming.

3½ tablespoons butter
1 cup sliced mushrooms
½ cup finely chopped Walla Walla sweet or
    red Bermuda onion
½ cup chopped ham
4 hard-cooked eggs, peeled
2 tablespoons chopped parsley
2 tablespoons flour
1 cup milk

½ cup sour cream
1 tablespoon Dijon mustard
1½ teaspoons raspberry mustard or coarse-
    grained mustard
1 cup freshly grated Swiss cheese
6 plain or corn "Australian" toaster
    biscuits or English muffins
4 Roma tomatoes, diced

In a large skillet over medium heat, melt 2 tablespoons of the butter. Add the mushrooms, onion, and ham; saute until the onion and mushrooms are limp. Set aside.

In a small bowl mash the egg yolks with the parsley. In another small bowl dice the egg whites. Set both bowls aside.

In a large saucepan over medium heat, melt the remaining 1½ tablespoons butter. When it starts to bubble, sprinkle in the flour. Stir in the milk until the mixture thickens. Add

the sour cream, mustards, and cheese; stir until blended. Add the reserved sauteed mushroom mixture and the diced egg whites. Reduce the heat to low, cover, and keep warm.

Preheat the broiler. Split the biscuits and broil until golden. Place a heaping tablespoonful of the diced tomatoes on top of each biscuit, then cover with the warm cheese mixture. Sprinkle with the egg-yolk mixture; serve hot.

# *U*PTOWN SCRAMBLED EGGS

### SERVES 6

12 eggs, beaten
3 tablespoons half-and-half
1 teaspoooon seasoned salt, or more to taste
2 teaspoons dried dill weed
4 tablespoons butter
⅔ cup sliced mushrooms
½ cup thinly sliced green onion

½ pound bulk Italian sausage, cooked and crumbled
6 croissants, sliced partway through lengthwise
Salt and pepper, to taste
8 ounces cream cheese, chilled and cut into small cubes

Preheat the oven to 350°F. In a large bowl combine the eggs, half-and-half, seasoned salt, and dill. Beat until well combined, then set aside.

In a large skillet over medium heat, melt the butter. Add the mushrooms and green onion; saute until limp. Add the sausage and cook until it starts to sizzle. Meanwhile, place the croissants open face on a baking sheet in the oven.

To the sizzling sausage in the skillet, add the reserved egg mixture and the salt and pepper; cook until the eggs are set but still soft (or to the degree of doneness you prefer). Remove from the heat and gently fold in the cream cheese. Do not return the pan to the heat; the cream cheese should not cook into the eggs.

Remove the warm croissants from the oven and spoon the egg mixture onto the bottom of each. Fold the top of each croissant over the filling and serve immediately.

# SPINACH QUICHE

SERVES 4 TO 6

2 tablespoons butter
½ cup finely chopped onion
1 package (10 ounces) frozen chopped
    spinach, cooked and well drained
1½ cups freshly grated Jarlsberg cheese
3 eggs, beaten
¾ cup milk
1 teaspoon garlic powder

1 teaspoon salt
1 teaspoon dried basil
½ teaspoon celery salt
1 unbaked pie shell (10 inches), edges
    crimped decoratively
½ cup freshly grated Romano or Parmesan
    cheese

Preheat the oven to 400°F. In a large skillet over medium heat, melt the butter. Add the onion and saute until limp, then add the spinach and stir to combine. Remove from the heat.

In a large bowl combine the Jarlsberg cheese, eggs, milk, garlic powder, salt, basil, and celery salt. Stir in the spinach mixture, then pour into the pie shell. Top with the Romano cheese. Bake for 15 minutes, then reduce the heat to 350°F and continue baking until the quiche is set (about 20 minutes longer).

# COUNTRY INN APPLE PECAN PANCAKES WITH APPLE CIDER SYRUP

SERVES 4

2 cups flour
1 teaspoon baking powder
½ teaspoon salt
½ teaspoon ground cinnamon
1 teaspoon granulated sugar
1½ cups buttermilk

2 eggs, beaten
1 cup chopped pecans
2 large Golden Delicious apples, peeled,
   cored, and grated
1 tablespoon vegetable oil

APPLE CIDER SYRUP

1 tablespoon butter
1 teaspoon ground cinnamon
1 tablespoon brown sugar

1 cup apple cider or apple juice
1 tablespoon cornstarch dissolved in
   2 tablespoons cider or juice

In a medium bowl whisk together the flour, baking powder, salt, cinnamon, and granulated sugar. Add the buttermilk and eggs; stir until the batter is smooth. Fold in the nuts and apples. Set aside.

In a large skillet over medium heat, warm the oil. Ladle a heaping serving spoon of batter into the skillet and cook until the top and middle of the pancake are set, then turn and cook until the other side is golden. Repeat for each pancake. Serve with the Apple Cider Syrup on the side.

*Apple Cider Syrup:* In a small saucepan over medium heat, melt the butter. Whisk in the cinnamon and brown sugar. Add the cider and heat through. Add the cornstarch mixture and cook, stirring, until the sauce has thickened and turned shiny and clear.

# $\mathcal{L}$EMON PANCAKES WITH FRESH LEMON SYRUP

### SERVES 4 TO 6

2 cups buttermilk pancake mix
2 cups milk
1 egg

FRESH LEMON SYRUP

3 cups water
2 cups sugar

1 tablespoon vegetable oil
2 tablespoons sugar
Zest and juice of 2 lemons

1 cup lemon juice
1 tablespoon freshly grated lemon zest

In a large bowl combine all the ingredients; beat well. Ladle by large spoonfuls onto a hot, greased griddle. Cook until the pancakes bubble and the edges are set, then turn over with a spatula and cook until the other side is set. Serve with the warm syrup on the side.

*Fresh Lemon Syrup:* In a medium saucepan combine all the ingredients; bring to a boil, then reduce the heat and simmer until the syrup has thickened and been reduced by one-third (at least 20 minutes).

---

### A LESSON ON LEMONS

When choosing lemons, look for those that have a smooth, thin skin. They should also feel heavy, which means they are full of juice. You can keep lemons at room temperature for about a week, or in a plastic bag in the refrigerator for about a month.

The fastest, easiest way to remove the zest (the yellow part of the peel, not the white pith beneath it) is with a vegetable peeler. To mince the zest, place it in an electric coffee grinder (of course, you've cleaned out all the old grounds!), and grind until finely chopped. You can store any excess zest in a plastic bag in the freezer. That way, when a recipe calls for zest, you have it at your fingertips.

When juicing a lemon, have it at room temperature. Even better, heat it in the microwave for about 20 seconds. Then before juicing the lemon, roll it back and forth on a flat surface, mashing it gently with your hand. One medium lemon will produce about 3 tablespoons juice.

# HAZELNUT WAFFLES

MAKES ABOUT 8 WAFFLES

If you have any hazelnut liqueur or hazelnut syrup (like that used in espresso shops for *lattes* and Italian sodas), splash some in the maple syrup before serving. It's delicious!

½ cup warm water
1 package active dry yeast
1 cup milk, warmed
1½ cups hazelnut-flavored coffee creamer
8 tablespoons butter, melted
1 teaspoon salt

1 teaspoon sugar
2 cups flour
2 eggs
¼ teaspoon baking soda
1¼ cups chopped hazelnuts
Maple syrup, for accompaniment

Place the water in the largest mixing bowl you have (the batter will rise a lot). Sprinkle in the yeast; stir until it dissolves. Let stand for 5 minutes, then add the milk, coffee creamer, butter, salt, sugar, and flour; beat until smooth. Cover with plastic wrap and let stand overnight.

The next morning beat in the eggs, baking soda, and 1 cup of the hazelnuts (reserve ¼ cup for garnish). Pour ½ to ¾ cup of the batter onto a hot waffle iron. Cook until the waffle is golden and crisp. Keep warm. Repeat with the remaining batter. Garnish each waffle with the reserved chopped hazelnuts and serve with the maple syrup.

# STUFFED FRENCH TOAST WITH FRESH PEACHES

SERVES 4

I can't wait until peach season to prepare this dish. It's also very good with nectarines. In winter you can use frozen peaches; just heat them in a saucepan, add lemon juice and sugar, then thicken with a little cornstarch. This is an excellent breakfast for carbo-loading before a day of skiing!

6 eggs, beaten
1 cup half-and-half
¾ cup granulated sugar
1 teaspoon ground cinnamon
1 teaspoon almond extract
6 fresh peaches, peeled and sliced
Juice of 1 large lemon

8 ounces cream cheese, at room
   temperature
4 tablespoons butter, for skillet
8 slices bread of your choice
Confectioners' sugar, for sprinkling
Maple syrup, for accompaniment

In a large bowl beat together the eggs, half-and-half, 3 tablespoons of the granulated sugar, the cinnamon, and almond extract; set aside.

In another large bowl combine the peaches with the remaining granulated sugar and the lemon juice. Remove ¾ cup of the peach mixture and mash with a fork; combine with the cream cheese and set aside.

In a large skillet over medium heat, melt the butter. Meanwhile, soak each slice of bread in the reserved egg mixture, then saute in the melted butter until the bread is golden on each side.

Arrange 4 slices of the French toast on a serving platter. Spoon ¼ cup of the reserved cream cheese mixture onto each slice and spread until it is evenly distributed. Cover each with another slice of French toast. Top with the peach mixture and sprinkle with the confectioners' sugar. Serve with the maple syrup.

# $\mathscr{H}$ERBED CREPES PARISIENNE

MAKES 16 MEDIUM CREPES, 8 SERVINGS

3 eggs
2 cups flour
1½ cups milk
1 cup chicken stock
4 tablespoons butter, melted
½ teaspoon dried tarragon

FILLING

2 tablespoons butter
½ pound mushrooms, sliced
3 tablespoons minced green onion
1 cup cubed ham
Salt and pepper, to taste
12 ounces cream cheese

Butter, for pan and casserole
6 tablespoons butter, melted
3 tablespoons freshly grated Parmesan
   cheese
2 tablespoons each chopped parsley and
   fresh chives

2¼ cups sour cream
3 tablespoons freshly grated Parmesan
   cheese
2 tablespoons minced fresh dill or 1
   tablespoon dried dill weed

To prepare the crepes, in the container of a blender combine the eggs, flour, milk, stock, the 4 tablespoons melted butter, and the tarragon; process until smooth. Let the batter rest for at least 30 minutes.

Place a crepe pan or large nonstick skillet over medium heat; brush the surface with the butter. Pour in a ladle full of crepe batter and immediately begin swirling the batter around the pan until it covers the bottom evenly. Cook until the crepe begins to bubble up and the sides begin to crisp, then flip the crepe and cook for about another 30 seconds. Remove from the pan and keep warm. Repeat with the remaining batter.

Preheat the oven to 325°F. Butter a large casserole dish and set aside. Prepare the Filling. Arrange the warm crepes on a flat work surface and divide the Filling evenly among them. Roll up each crepe, then place them seam side down in the prepared dish. Drizzle lightly with the 6 tablespoons melted butter and bake for 25 minutes.

Combine the cheese, parsley, and chives; sprinkle onto the crepes and serve.

*Filling:* In a crepe pan or 10-inch skillet over medium heat, melt the butter. Add the mushrooms, green onion, and ham; cook until the mushrooms are soft. Drain off any mushroom liquid, then season the mushroom mixture with the salt and pepper; set aside.

In a medium mixing bowl, combine the cream cheese and sour cream; mix until smooth. Add the reserved mushroom mixture, Parmesan cheese, and dill; mix well.

# ICICLE RIVER SALMON TART

SERVES 4

This is one of my favorite breakfast offerings. It whips up in a jiffy and looks elegant. I find that even people who are "iffy" on fish warm up to this dish in a hurry. It's also perfect for lunch when served with Spinach and Apple Salad and croissants.

2 tablespoons butter
½ cup sliced mushrooms
¼ cup chopped onion
¼ cup chopped red or yellow bell pepper (optional)
½ cup mayonnaise
2 tablespoons flour
2 eggs, beaten
½ cup half-and-half
8 ounces Swiss cheese, grated

4 ounces cream cheese, cut into small cubes
1 can (14¾ ounces) salmon, drained and picked over for bones
2 teaspoons dried dill weed
¼ teaspoon ground black pepper
2 tablespoons freshly grated Parmesan cheese
2 teaspoons sour cream, for topping
4 sprigs fresh dill weed or parsley, for garnish

Preheat the oven to 350°F. In a large skillet over medium heat, melt the butter. Add the mushrooms, onion, and bell pepper (if desired); saute until soft. Set aside to cool.

In a medium bowl combine the mayonnaise, flour, eggs, half-and-half, Swiss cheese, cream cheese, salmon, dill, and ground pepper. Stir in the cooled mushroom mixture. Pour into a greased quiche or tart pan, sprinkle with the Parmesan cheese, and bake until puffed and golden (about 20 minutes). Cut into 4 pieces and top each serving with ½ teaspoon sour cream; garnish with a sprig of fresh dill.

# ST. PATRICK'S POTATO HASH

## SERVES 6

Being Irish, I've never met a potato I didn't like, but this is my favorite potato dish. Spicy and hearty, it's a real crowd pleaser! I'm thrilled when there are leftovers. When cooking for vegetarians, simply leave out the sausage.

8 eggs
3 pounds red-skinned potatoes, cut into ¼- to ½-inch cubes
5 to 6 tablespoons olive oil
1 large yellow onion, peeled and chopped
1 large red bell pepper, seeded and chopped
1 large yellow bell pepper, seeded and chopped
2 cups chopped kielbasa

2 teaspoons salt
1 teaspoon ground black pepper
1 tablespoon dried oregano
1 tablespoon dried basil
3 tablespoons minced parsley
1 cup freshly grated sharp Cheddar cheese
¼ cup chopped parsley, for sprinkling
Salsa, catsup, and sour cream, for accompaniment

Poach the eggs and set aside. Preheat the oven to 450°F. In a large stockpot of boiling salted water, cook the potatoes until just tender when pierced with a fork. Remove from the water and drain.

Meanwhile, in a large skillet over medium heat, warm the oil. Add the onion, bell peppers, and sausage; saute until the onion is limp. Add the drained potatoes, salt, ground pepper, oregano, and basil. Saute until the potatoes are cooked through (about 5 minutes).

Remove the pan from the heat and stir in the 3 tablespoons parsley. Top with the reserved poached eggs and sprinkle with the grated cheese. Pop into the oven until the cheese melts. Remove from the oven, sprinkle with the ¼ cup parsley, and serve with the salsa, catsup, and sour cream.

# Appetizers

# COUNTRY FARMHOUSE FONDUE

SERVES 4

Fondue is a wonderful fall and winter appetizer. It also lends itself to a romantic dinner in front of a fire. For a superb meal, serve the fondue with a small salad, a bottle of wine, and a simple dessert.

1 pound Gouda cheese, grated
2 tablespoons flour
1 cup apple cider
1 clove garlic, peeled and finely minced
Freshly grated nutmeg, to taste

4 to 6 crisp, firm apples, peeled and sliced, for dipping
Large cubes toasted French bread, for dipping

In a large bowl combine the grated cheese and flour; set aside. In a medium saucepan or an enameled pot, heat the cider. Add the garlic and stir slowly. Blend in the reserved cheese mixture a little at a time, stirring constantly until the fondue is velvety smooth. Sprinkle with the nutmeg.

Transfer the mixture to a fondue pot and place it over a flame to keep warm. Serve with the apple slices and bread cubes for dipping.

# $\mathcal{B}$ABY RED-SKINNED POTATOES
## WITH
## SUN-DRIED TOMATO CREAM FILLING
### SERVES 2 OR 3

½ pound baby red-skinned potatoes, or more as needed

4 ounces cream cheese or mild goat cheese, such as Montrachet, at room temperature

2 tablespoons drained and minced oil-packed sun-dried tomatoes

1 tablespoon thinly sliced green onion

In a vegetable steamer, steam the potatoes until tender when pierced. Remove from the heat and let cool just enough to handle. Cut in half and place cut side down on a serving tray. With a melon baller, spoon out some of the top of the potato to form a small depression.

In a small bowl whip together the cream cheese, tomatoes, and green onion, reserving some chunks of tomato for garnish. Fill each potato cavity with a dollop of the creamy mixture, then garnish with the tomato.

> *We may live without friends, we may live without books, but civilized man cannot live without cooks.*
> —Edward Robert-Bulwer-Lytton
> (1831–1891)

# CHINESE BARBECUED PORK

SERVES 4 TO 6

1 pork tenderloin (about 2 pounds)
2 cloves garlic, peeled and minced
¼-inch slice fresh ginger
3 teaspoons sugar
1 teaspoon salt
1 tablespoon dry sherry

3 tablespoons soy sauce
2½ generous tablespoons honey
½ teaspoon Chinese five-spice powder
   (see Note)
Chinese hot mustard, for accompaniment
Sesame seeds, for accompaniment

Pierce the tenderloin with a fork; set aside. In a baking pan combine the garlic, fresh ginger, sugar, salt, sherry, soy sauce, honey, and five-spice powder. Add the tenderloin and let it marinate for 24 hours, turning occasionally.

Preheat the oven to 325°F. Roast the tenderloin in the marinade until no longer pink (25 to 30 minutes), basting with the marinade and pan drippings. Remove from the oven and transfer to a platter. Serve with the hot mustard and sesame seeds.

*Note:* Chinese five-spice powder is found in the ethnic food section or seasonings section of well-stocked supermarkets. It's actually a blend of six spices: star anise, cinnamon, cloves, fennel, ginger, and licorice root. Each of these spices taken on its own is a strong flavor; the combination is potent but fabulous. Use the blend sparingly, but find many uses for it.

# CLAM PUFFS

SERVES 4

8 ounces cream cheese, at room
   temperature
3 tablespoons mayonnaise
3 tablespoons dry sherry

½ teaspoon Tabasco Sauce
2 green onions, thinly sliced
1 can (6½ ounces) minced clams, drained
1 sourdough baguette, sliced and toasted

Preheat the broiler. In a large bowl combine the cream cheese and mayonnaise. Stir in the sherry and Tabasco. Fold in the green onions and minced clams. Spread the mixture onto the toasted baguette slices and broil until bubbly and golden.

*Variation:* Cook and drain 1 package (10 ounces) frozen artichoke hearts (not marinated) according to package directions. Spoon the clam mixture onto each artichoke heart and place under the broiler until bubbly.

# CHEVRE AND GREEN GRAPES

SERVES 4 TO 6

When I serve these I usually make more than the recipe calls for, since I eat half of them before they're ever served!

¼ cup mild goat cheese, such as Montrachet
¼ to ½ teaspoon half-and-half or whipping cream

20 large seedless green grapes
½ cup chopped pistachios or pecans

In a small bowl combine the goat cheese and half-and half; blend until smooth. With your fingers evenly coat each grape with the cheese mixture. Place the coated grapes on a baking sheet and chill until set, then roll the grapes in the chopped nuts.

# WALNUT AND STILTON GRAPES

SERVES 4 TO 6

For a creative presentation, save the stems from the grapes and mound the fruit around the stems to look like a bunch of grapes on the vine. It takes extra time, but it's impressive.

¼ pound Stilton cheese, crumbled
3 ounces cream cheese, at room
   temperature

20 large red seedless grapes
½ cup finely chopped walnuts

In a small bowl blend together the Stilton and cream cheese. With your fingers evenly coat each grape with the cheese mixture. Place the coated grapes on a baking sheet and chill until set, then roll the grapes in the chopped nuts.

# TIPSY CRAB

SERVES 4

If you like garlic, this is the dish for you! The savory broth is memorable.
Serve the crab with loads of crusty French bread to soak up the broth, and
provide bibs for your guests (cracking the crabs can get a bit messy). This
dish also makes a wonderful entree: serve it with Fresh and Lovely Herb
Salad and complete the meal with the Lemon Tart.

8 tablespoons butter
1 cup dry vermouth
1 can (10¾ ounces) chicken stock
2 tablespoons chopped parsley
4 cloves garlic, peeled and minced
1 tablespoon soy sauce

1½ tablespoons freshly squeezed lemon
  juice
1 teaspoon sugar
2 medium Dungeness crabs, cooked,
  cleaned, and cracked

In a large kettle or stockpot over medium heat, melt the butter. Gradually stir in the vermouth and stock. Add the parsley, garlic, soy sauce, lemon juice, and sugar. Bring to a boil, then reduce the heat, cover, and simmer for 15 minutes.

To the hot broth, add the cracked crabs and simmer until the crabs are just heated through (10 to 15 minutes). The crabs should not be cooked again, just heated.

Divide the crabs among serving bowls and ladle the broth over top.

# WALLA WALLA SWEET ONION
## AND
# OREGON BLUE CHEESE TART
## WITH HAZELNUT CRUST

SERVES 6 TO 8

4 tablespoons butter
4 medium Walla Walla sweet onions,
    peeled and thinly sliced
4 eggs
½ cup sour cream
½ cup half-and-half or heavy cream

1 tablespoon minced fresh dill or
    ½ teaspoon dried dill weed
½ teaspoon Dijon mustard
6 to 8 ounces Oregon blue cheese,
    crumbled
Freshly grated Parmesan cheese, for
    sprinkling

CRUST

½ cup skinned and chopped hazelnuts
1¾ cups flour
½ teaspoon salt
8 tablespoons butter, cut into small cubes

2 teaspoons minced fresh dill weed
2 eggs, beaten
2 tablespoons ice water

Prepare the Crust and chill as directed. To prepare the filling, melt the butter in a large skillet over medium-low heat. Add the onions and saute until they carmelize (at least 25 minutes). The long cooking makes the onions even sweeter.

Meanwhile, in a large bowl combine the eggs, sour cream, half-and-half, dill, and mustard. Set aside.

Preheat the oven to 375°F. On a well-floured work surface, roll out the chilled Crust to ⅛ inch thick. Place it in a tart pan with a removable bottom, or use a pie plate. Trim the dough and crimp the edges decoratively. Freeze for 1 hour.

Partially bake the tart shell for 8 to 10 minutes. Remove from the oven and let cool slightly. Reduce the heat to 350°F. Fill the tart shell with the carmelized onions, then sprinkle with the blue cheese. Very carefully pour the reserved egg mixture over the onions and cheese. Sprinkle with the Parmesan. Place the tart on a baking sheet and bake until lightly browned and set (25 to 35 minutes). Let stand for 10 minutes before serving.

*Crust:* In the work bowl of a food processor, grind the hazelnuts. Add the flour and salt. Drop in the butter a little at a time, then add the dill, eggs, and ice water; process until a ball of dough is formed. Enclose the dough in plastic wrap and chill.

# OYSTERS IN A CRAB QUILT

### SERVES 4

1 jar (10 to 12 ounces) small oysters or 1
 dozen small oysters, shucked and cleaned

FILLING

| | |
|---|---|
| 4 tablespoons butter | ½ teaspoon ground white pepper |
| ⅓ cup thinly sliced green onion | 1½ tablespoons flour |
| ⅓ cup thinly sliced mushrooms | 1 pound fresh Dungeness crab, cooked, |
| ¼ cup finely chopped red bell pepper | cleaned, shelled, and picked over for |
| 1 clove garlic, peeled and finely chopped | shell fragments |
| 1 teaspoon finely chopped cilantro | Salt, to taste |
| 1¼ cups creme fraiche, at room | |
| temperature | |

TOPPING

1 cup seasoned bread crumbs
4 tablespoons butter
1 tablespoon chopped parsley

3 tablespoons freshly grated Parmesan
 cheese

Grease escargot dishes, gratin dishes, or sea shells; place 4 oysters in each dish and chill.

Prepare the Filling and Topping; set aside. Preheat the oven to 350°F.

Spoon the Filling over the oysters and sprinkle with the Topping. Bake until the Topping is crispy brown and bubbly (about 30 minutes).

*Filling:* In a large skillet over medium-high heat, melt 2 tablespoons of the butter. Add the green onion, mushrooms, bell pepper,

garlic, and cilantro; saute until soft (6 to 10 minutes). Remove from the heat and add the creme fraiche and ground pepper; stir until all the ingredients are thoroughly combined.

In a small skillet over medium-low heat, prepare a roux *(see Note)* with the remaining 2 tablespoons butter and the flour. Stir the roux into the mushroom mixture in the large skillet. Return that skillet to medium-low heat and cook, stirring constantly, until the creme fraiche begins to thicken (about 5 minutes). Stir in the crabmeat and cook until the crab is just heated through. Add the salt.

*Topping:* Combine all the ingredients and mix well.

*Note:* Roux is a simply a sauce thickener. Made from flour and butter, it is cooked over low to medium heat until the flour just barely begins to turn a light golden. It's important to cook the roux to remove the flour taste, and to activate the starch in the flour so that it will begin to absorb the liquid you stir it into. This absorption will thicken the sauce.

> *Greengrocers rise at dawn of sun*
> *August the fifth—come haste away*
> *To Billingsgate the thousands run*
> *'Tis Oyster Day! 'Tis Oyster Day!*
> —From the
> **Every-Day Book by Hone, 1829**

# SIMPLE AND SIMPLY WONDERFUL CROSTINI

MAKES 12 CROSTINI

*Crostini* are little Italian appetizers. Authentic *crostini* began as humble fare—grilled bread rubbed with garlic and olive oil. As the popularity grew, all sorts of variations have arisen. This is a delicious variation on a very old classic.

1 cup chopped fresh basil
4 Roma tomatoes, chopped
3 yellow pear tomatoes, chopped (if unavailable, use all Roma tomatoes)
2 cloves garlic, peeled and minced
12 to 15 Kalamata olives, pitted and coarsely chopped

¾ cup freshly grated Asiago cheese
Salt and freshly ground pepper, to taste
1 sourdough baguette, cut into ¼ inch slices

Preheat the broiler. In a large bowl combine all the ingredients except the baguette. Place the baguette slices on a baking sheet and spread each with 1½ teaspoons (or more to taste) of the tomato mixture. Broil until the *crostini* are golden brown and the cheese is bubbly (2 to 3 minutes). Serve warm.

*How do they taste? They taste like more.*
—H. L. Mencken (1880–1956)

# Salads

# ABBIE'S ITALIAN RICE SALAD

SERVES 6 TO 8

6 cups cooked white rice
1 cup chopped red bell pepper
1 cup chopped yellow or orange bell
    pepper
1 cup chopped Walla Walla sweet onion or
    red Bermuda onion
1 cup quartered marinated artichoke hearts

½ cup chopped parsley
⅓ cup minced fresh dill weed
½ cup golden raisins
⅓ cup sliced black olives
2½ cups cubed cooked chicken or turkey
    breast meat
1 cup chopped dry Italian salami

GARLIC VINAIGRETTE DRESSING

1 cup vegetable oil
¾ cup white wine vinegar
2 teaspoons salt
2 teaspoons freshly ground black pepper
1 tablespoon minced garlic

1½ teaspoons chopped fresh basil or
    ½ teaspoon dried basil
1½ teaspoons chopped fresh oregano or
    ½ teaspoon dried oregano
⅓ cup chopped parsley

Prepare the Garlic Vinaigrette Dressing
and chill as directed. In a large bowl
gently toss the salad ingredients together.
Top with the vinaigrette dressing and toss
again. Let the salad marinate overnight.

*Garlic Vinaigrette Dressing:* Combine all the
ingredients in the container of a blender.
Mix well, then chill.

# DON'T FORGET TO STOP AND EAT THE FLOWERS

Edible landscaping makes you really shine, in the yard as well as in the kitchen! Flowers add a special glamour and surprise to any dish. Most of the flowers we grow here at Cashmere Country Inn are edible. I garnish the plates with them, add them to salads, and sprinkle them on top of entrees and desserts. Every spring I wait eagerly for the first flowers to pop out from beneath the snow. As much as I enjoy the winter, I always feel as though my heart's received a jump start when I take in the fresh colors of spring.

Here is a selection of some of my favorite edible flowers. Don't be afraid to use any of these when you're cooking. They are a delightful addition to salads, changing them from basic to beautiful. Some of these flowers are used more for their aesthetic appeal and don't have much flavor, such as the Johnny-jump-up; others provide wonderful flavor as well as beauty, such as nasturtiums, borage, and tuberous begonia (which has a lemony flavor).

The next time you're at a nursery selecting flowers, remember you can have a wide range of color in your food as well as in your yard by choosing some of the following. Use only the flowers (not the leaves) unless otherwise indicated.

| | | |
|---|---|---|
| Tuberous begonia (leaves and flowers) | Geranium | Nasturtium (leaves and flowers) |
| Borage | Hollyhock | |
| Calendula | Honeysuckle | Pansy |
| Chrysanthemum | Jasmine | Poppy |
| Clary sage | Johnny-jump-up | Rose |
| Daylily | Lavender | Tulip |
| English daisy | Lemon Gem marigold | Violet |
| | Lilac | |

Most of these flowers are perennials or self-seeding annuals. With calendula and borage, once you have some, you'll never get rid of them! Many of the plants listed grow like weeds, and are surprisingly easy to maintain.

Try pansies and nasturtiums in a salad for a peppery, watercress-like flavor; or add a blue star-shaped flower from borage for a cucumber flavor. For a lovely garnish on desserts, sprinkle with petals of lavender, violets, or roses. With roses, use the most fragrant petals you can find; the greater the fragrance, the richer the flavor.

# BEVY'S BROCCOLI SALAD

### SERVES 4

1 pound thinly sliced bacon
½ cup mayonnaise
½ cup sour cream
⅓ cup sugar, or to taste
2½ tablespoons red wine vinegar
1 large head broccoli, divided into florets, tough skin and ends trimmed

1 medium red Bermuda onion, peeled and chopped
½ cup salted sunflower seeds
½ cup golden raisins

In a large skillet over medium heat, fry the bacon until crisp. Drain, let cool, and crumble, then set aside.

In a small bowl combine the mayonnaise, sour cream, sugar, and vinegar. In a large bowl combine the broccoli, onion, sunflower seeds, raisins, and the crumbled bacon. Pour the mayonnaise mixture over the broccoli mixture and stir until blended. Chill before serving.

# FRESH AND LOVELY HERB SALAD

### SERVES 4 TO 6

4 cups romaine lettuce torn into bite-sized
    pieces
4 cups *mesclun* (mixed lettuces) torn into
    bite-sized pieces
1 cup chopped fresh mint

RASPBERRY VINAIGRETTE

2 tablespoons raspberry vinegar
2 tablespoons orange juice
1 teaspoon honey mustard
¼ teaspoon salt

1 cup chopped fresh basil
⅓ cup thinly sliced green onion
¼ cup edible flower petals, such as violets,
    nasturtiums, pansies, and borage
½ cup chopped roasted hazelnuts

½ teaspoon sugar
¼ teaspoon freshly ground black pepper
6 tablespoons salad oil

Prepare the Raspberry Vinaigrette and set aside. In a large salad bowl, combine all the greens, herbs, and nuts. Pour the dressing over the salad and toss lightly until coated.

*Raspberry Vinaigrette:* In a small bowl combine the vinegar, orange juice, mustard, salt, sugar, and ground pepper. Gradually whisk in the oil until thoroughly blended.

# THE PERFECT GREEK SALAD

### SERVES 4

I'm of the philosophy that in a really good Greek salad you can never have too many olives or feta cheese. You may want to cut my amounts back a bit, although in my opinion (as you can tell by the title), I think this salad is perfect the way it is! Do try to use Greek oregano; it is more pungent and has a richer flavor than ordinary oregano. One of the herbs in my yard I couldn't do without, it is a stunning border plant in the landscape, and it grows profusely.

½ head romaine lettuce, shredded
1 cucumber, peeled and diced
1 green bell pepper, seeded and diced
½ cup diced onion
1 large tomato, diced

¾ cup Kalamata olives
10 ounces feta cheese, crumbled
⅔ cup good-quality Italian dressing
¾ teaspoon dried Greek oregano
½ teaspoon freshly ground black pepper

In a large salad bowl, combine the lettuce, cucumber, bell pepper, onion, tomato, and olives. Sprinkle with the feta cheese. In a small bowl whisk the salad dressing with the oregano and ground pepper. Pour over the salad and toss well.

# $\mathscr{M}$ING'S SHREDDED CHICKEN SALAD

### SERVES 4

I grew up in the San Francisco Bay area, where Chinese food was plentiful and usually always good. But Ming's had the best. I remember going there for special occasions and always having their chicken salad as the center of many wonderful multicourse meals. After living in Washington for a few years, I went back to California and made it a point to eat at Ming's. They gave me this recipe and I treasure it, as they closed a short time later. Now whenever I'm nostalgic for my childhood, at least I can still have a taste of Ming's.

½ cup cornstarch
½ cup tapioca flour *(see Note)*
1 large fryer chicken (3 to 4 pounds)
Oil, for frying chicken
1 tablespoon Chinese mustard, or more to taste
½ teaspoon sesame oil
¼ teaspoon Chinese five-spice powder *(see Note)*

1 cup finely shredded iceberg lettuce
½ bunch cilantro
3 green onions, sliced lengthwise into slivers
½ cup peanut oil
1 cup fried rice vermicelli *(see Note)*
1 tablespoon toasted sesame seeds
1½ tablespoons chopped almonds

In a small bowl combine the cornstarch and tapioca flour. Pat it on the chicken, coating it completely. Cook the whole chicken in a steamer for 50 to 60 minutes. Let cool, then split the chicken in half. Deep fry it until the skin is a golden, crispy brown.

Debone the chicken by filleting and shredding the meat with the grain (not across the grain). Place the chicken strips in a large bowl and add the Chinese mustard, sesame

oil, five-spice powder, lettuce, cilantro, green onions, and peanut oil. Mix thoroughly.

Mound the vermicelli on a serving platter, top with the chicken mixture, and sprinkle with the sesame seeds and almonds.

*Note:* You can find tapioca flour and fried rice vermicelli at Asian markets. Chinese five-spice powder is available in Asian markets and well-stocked supermarkets.

# MINTY ORANGE SALAD

SERVES 4 TO 6

3 oranges
1 small clove garlic, peeled and finely
　chopped
¼ teaspoon salt
¼ teaspoon dry mustard
2 tablespoons rice vinegar

¼ cup olive oil
¼ teaspoon freshly ground black pepper
⅓ cup chopped fresh mint
1 large head red butter lettuce, torn into
　bite-sized pieces

Grate the zest of one of the oranges and reserve, then juice the same orange; reserve ¼ cup juice. Peel and section the other 2 oranges and set aside.

In a salad bowl combine the garlic, salt, and mustard. Add the vinegar and reserved orange juice. Whisk in the olive oil and ground pepper. Add the mint, lettuce, and reserved orange sections; toss well. Sprinkle with the reserved orange zest.

# ASIAN CABBAGE SALAD

SERVES 6 TO 8

1 package "Oriental-flavored" Ramen
    noodles (reserve seasoning package for
    Dressing)
1 large head cabbage, shredded

4 green onions, sliced
½ cup slivered almonds, toasted
3 tablespoons sesame seeds, toasted

DRESSING

½ cup vegetable oil
3 tablespoons red wine vinegar
3 tablespoons sugar
1 teaspoon MSG (optional)

½ teaspoon salt
¼ teaspoon ground black pepper
Seasoning package from Ramen noodles

With a rolling pin crush the noodles into small chunks. Place them in a large bowl and add the cabbage, green onions, almonds, and sesame seeds. Prepare the Dressing; pour it over the cabbage mixture and combine until well blended and the cabbage is coated with Dressing. Serve immediately.

*Dressing:* Mix together all the ingredients and chill. Stir occasionally; it will thicken as it sets.

# PEAR, CANDIED PECAN, AND OREGON BLUE CHEESE SALAD

SERVES 6

This may sound like an odd combination, but at one of our "taste test" dinner parties, this was among the favorite salads. The peppery flavor of the watercress combined with the sweetness of the nuts and richness of the blue cheese is a hard combination to beat. For the best flavor, prepare this salad as close to serving time as possible.

2 cups chopped watercress leaves (no stems)
4 cups *mesclun* (mixed lettuces) torn into bite-sized pieces

2 ripe pears, peeled and thinly sliced
½ cup crumbled Oregon blue cheese

CANDIED PECANS

2 tablespoons sugar
1 tablespoon hot water

½ cup pecan halves

SHALLOT DRESSING

2 tablespoons lemon juice
½ cup olive oil
1 large shallot, peeled and minced

½ teaspoon sugar
½ teaspoon ground black pepper

Prepare the Candied Pecans and Shallot Dressing. In a large bowl combine the watercress, *mesclun*, pears, and Candied Pecans. Add the Shallot Dressing and mix gently. Divide among 6 salad plates or serve in a large bowl. Sprinkle with the blue cheese.

*Candied Pecans:* Pour the sugar into a small skillet over medium heat. Shake the pan until the sugar melts and turns golden. Stir in the hot water (the sugar will set up again, so keep it on the heat until it melts). Add the pecan halves and stir until they are entirely coated. Transfer the nuts to a piece of aluminum foil and let cool until they harden. Chop coarsely.

*Shallot Dressing:* Combine all the ingredients and mix well.

# SMOKED TROUT CAESAR SALAD WITH GARLIC CROUTONS

SERVES 6

2 whole fresh trout (10 to 12 ounces each), rinsed and patted dry
¼ cup coarse salt
2 quarts water
Mesquite or hickory chips, for barbecuing

DRESSING

1 clove garlic, peeled
3 eggs
2½ cups olive oil
½ cup freshly squeezed lemon juice

GARLIC CROUTONS

8 tablespoons butter
2 cloves garlic, peeled and minced

3 sprigs fresh rosemary
2 heads romaine lettuce, shredded into bite-sized pieces
½ cup freshly grated Parmesan cheese

1 tablespoon Worcestershire sauce
1 tube (3½ ounces) anchovy paste
1 teaspoon freshly ground black pepper

½ large loaf sourdough bread, cut into cubes

Prepare the Dressing and Garlic Croutons; set aside.

Place the trout in a 3-quart pan. Add the salt and water. The fish should be completely immersed in brine. Cover and refrigerate for 24 hours.

Place 2 to 3 handfuls mesquite chips in a basin of cold water; soak for 30 minutes. About an hour before serving the salad, build an indirect barbecue fire by placing the charcoal to one side of a kettle grill. When the charcoal becomes gray-white, drain the mesquite chips and toss them onto the fire. Oil the grill, cover the kettle, and leave the fire burn for 5 to 10 minutes.

Meanwhile, remove the trout from the brine. Drain, rinse under cold water, and pat dry with paper towels. With a sharp knife remove the heads. Butterfly the trout by making a slit down the center along the backbone on the inside. Place the trout, skin side down, on the grill away from the hot coals so that the fish cooks over indirect heat. Lay the rosemary sprigs on the fish. Cover the kettle and let the trout smoke until the flesh is cooked through (25 to 40 minutes). Remove from the grill, let cool, and pick the meat off the bones. Set aside.

Place the romaine in a large bowl and toss with as much Dressing as you like. (Store the extra in the refrigerator for future use.)

Gently stir in the trout. Sprinkle with the Garlic Croutons and Parmesan cheese.

*Dressing:* In the container of a blender, puree the garlic and eggs. Add the olive oil, lemon juice, Worcestershire sauce, anchovy paste, and ground pepper. Process until smooth, then chill.

*Garlic Croutons:* Preheat the oven to 250°F. In a large skillet over medium heat, melt the butter. Stir in the garlic. Add the bread cubes and toss until they are well coated. Place them on a baking sheet and bake, stirring occasionally, until the croutons are golden brown and crispy.

# SPINACH AND APPLE SALAD

## SERVES 6

We have an apple orchard full of Golden Delicious apple trees. I love to find new recipes to utilize apples in as many ways as possible. This is a nice change from a basic spinach salad.

2 pounds fresh spinach, rinsed and torn into bite-sized pieces
2 Golden Delicious apples, peeled, cored, and chopped

⅔ cup shelled roasted peanuts
½ cup sliced green onion
½ cup golden raisins
2 tablespoons sesame seeds, toasted

DRESSING

½ cup red wine vinegar
⅔ cup oil
2 to 3 tablespoons chutney
1 teaspoon curry powder

1 teaspoon salt
1 teaspoon dry mustard
¼ teaspoon Tabasco Sauce
½ teaspoon sugar

Prepare the Dressing and chill. Meanwhile, mix together the salad ingredients. Toss with the Dressing and serve immediately.

*Dressing:* Whisk together all the ingredients.

# Soups
# and
# Stews

❖

# $\mathcal{D}$ALE'S FAVORITE CLAM CHOWDER

### SERVES 6 TO 8

This makes a wonderfully rich and creamy soup, but it's not as thick as the traditional Boston clam chowder. If you prefer thick chowder, see *Note*. If you prefer a lower fat version, use buttermilk instead of the whipping cream, or a combination of the two. The buttermilk adds a nice tang and adds a fresh twist to an old favorite.

6 slices bacon, chopped
2 medium carrots, scraped and thinly sliced
2 stalks celery, thinly sliced
1 small onion, peeled and chopped
½ small red bell pepper, seeded and chopped
1 clove garlic, peeled and minced
1½ pounds red-skinned potatoes, peeled and cut into ½-inch cubes
2 bottles (8 ounces each) clam juice

8 cans (6 ounces each) minced clams, with liquid
1 bay leaf
½ teaspoon Tabasco Sauce
¼ teaspoon ground black pepper
1½ teaspoons Worcestershire sauce
¾ teaspoon dried thyme
½ teaspoon dried tarragon
4 cups whipping cream
Salt, to taste

$\mathbf{P}$lace the bacon in a stockpot over medium heat; cook until crisp. Remove and drain on paper towels.

Discard all but 2 tablespoons bacon drippings. To the pot add the carrots, celery, onion, bell pepper, and garlic; cook, stirring often, until the onion is limp. Add the potatos and clam juice; bring to a boil, reduce the heat to low, cover, and cook until the potatoes are tender when pierced (about

15 minutes). Stir in the clams and their liquid, bay leaf, Tabasco, ground pepper, Worcestershire, thyme, tarragon, whipping cream, and the drained bacon. Season with the salt. Heat until steaming, then serve.

*Note:* To thicken the chowder, add 2 tablespoons water to 2 to 3 tablespoons cornstarch, then add this to the chowder a little at a time. Stir frequently until you reach the desired thickness.

> *Chowder breathes reassurance. It breathes consolation.*
> —Clementine Paddleford (1900–1967)

# $\mathcal{M}$cINTOSH'S APPLE CHEDDAR BISQUE

SERVES 4

1 tablespoon olive oil
1 small onion, peeled and minced
1 stalk celery, finely chopped
1 small carrot, scraped and finely chopped
2 cloves garlic, peeled and minced
2 medium red-skinned potatoes, peeled
   and cut into ½-inch cubes
2 large McIntosh apples, peeled, cored,
   and cut into ½-inch cubes
2½ cups water

¾ cup dry white wine
½ teaspoon dried thyme
¾ teaspoon salt
¼ teaspoon freshly ground black pepper
¼ teaspoon cayenne pepper
½ cup half-and-half
1½ cups freshly grated sharp Cheddar
   cheese
2 teaspoons lemon juice

In a large saucepan or Dutch oven over medium heat, warm the oil. Add the onion and saute until limp (about 5 minutes). Add the celery, carrot, and garlic; saute 3 to 4 minutes. Stir in the potatoes, apples, water, wine, ¼ teaspoon of the thyme, the salt, ground pepper, and cayenne. Bring to a boil, then reduce the heat and simmer until the vegetables are very soft (about 40 minutes).

Transfer the mixture to the work bowl of a food processor or the container of a blender; puree until smooth. Strain through a sieve. Pour the mixture back into the pan; add the remaining ¼ teaspoon thyme, the half-and-half, and cheese. Heat until warmed through and the cheese is melted. Stir in the lemon juice and serve.

# MUSHROOM POTATO SOUP

### SERVES 4

1 cup diced red-skinned potatoes
¼ cup chopped celery
2 tablespoons minced onion
2 cups water
2 tablespoons butter
2 tablespoons flour
2 cups milk

½ pound mushrooms, sliced
1½ teaspoons salt
½ teaspoon celery salt
¼ teaspoon caraway seeds
½ teaspoon ground black pepper
1 tablespoon minced parsley

In a large saucepan over medium heat, cook the potatoes, celery, and onion in the water until tender. Remove from the heat (don't drain) and set aside.

In a stockpot or Dutch oven over medium heat, melt the butter. Blend in the flour to form a roux, stirring often. Add the potato mixture along with the liquid and cook until smooth. Stir in the milk, mushrooms, salt, celery salt, caraway, and ground pepper. Cook for 10 to 15 minutes. Stir in the parsley and serve hot.

> **Of soup and love, the first is best.**
> —Spanish proverb

# SPICY SEAFOOD GAZPACHO

SERVES 8

¼ cup olive oil
1 teaspoon lime juice
1 tablespoon red wine vinegar
1 red bell pepper, seeded and coarsely
  chopped
1 green bell pepper, seeded and coarsely
  chopped
4 medium tomatoes, seeded and coarsely
  chopped
1 medium Walla Walla sweet onion or red
  Bermuda onion, peeled and finely
  chopped

1 cucumber, peeled, seeded, and coarsely
  chopped
2 cloves garlic, peeled and finely chopped
2 cups tomato juice
¼ cup minced fresh chives
2 tablespoons minced cilantro
2 teaspoons Worcestershire sauce
½ teaspoon Tabasco Sauce
Salt and pepper, to taste
¾ cup cooked Dungeness crabmeat
¾ cup cooked shrimp meat

In a small bowl whisk together the oil, lime juice, and vinegar; set aside.

In the work bowl of a food processor, place half of the following: the red and green bell peppers, tomato, onion, cucumber, and garlic. Add the tomato juice; puree.

Transfer the puree to a large bowl and stir in the remaining bell peppers, tomato, onion, cucumber, and garlic. Add the reserved lime juice mixture, the chives, cilantro, Worcestershire, Tabasco, and salt and pepper.

Add the crab and shrimp (reserve a little for garnish) and toss gently. Cover and chill. Serve in chilled bowls, garnishing with the reserved seafood.

# SUMMERTIME WHITE GAZPACHO

## SERVES 4 TO 6

I prefer gazpacho a little crunchy, but you can make this very smooth instead. Try it both ways: smooth for a more sophisticated meal, chunky for a casual meal.

2 large English or hothouse cucumbers
3 green onions, thinly sliced
2 cloves garlic, peeled and minced
1 tablespoon chopped parsley
2 cups chicken stock
½ cup sour cream

3 tablespoons mayonnaise
2½ teaspoons rice vinegar
1 teaspoon salt
½ teaspoon freshly ground black pepper
½ cup chopped tomato, for garnish
¼ cup chopped fresh chives, for garnish

Peel and trim off the ends of the cucumbers. Cut the remaining cucumber in half lengthwise. With the tip of a teaspoon, scoop out the seeds from the center and discard. Cut the cucumber into chunks, and place them in the work bowl of a food processor or the container of a blender. Add the green onion, garlic, and parsley; blend the mixture to the desired smoothness. Add the chicken stock and process until blended.

In a large mixing bowl, combine the sour cream, mayonnaise, and vinegar. Blend well, then gradually stir in the cucumber mixture. Season to taste with the salt and ground pepper. Stir until the soup is well blended. Cover and chill.

Ladle the soup into individual bowls. Garnish with the chopped tomato and chives. Serve immediately.

# FRESH PEACH SOUP

SERVES 6 TO 8

This is a big hit with the guests, but I always get puzzled looks when I first serve it. Although quite common in Europe, fruit soup is still somewhat unusual in the United States. Once guests taste that first spoonful, however, they're hooked. The flavor is like an explosion of fresh peaches in your mouth!

**6 large ripe peaches, peeled and sliced**
**¼ cup lemon juice**
**½ cup sugar**
**1 cup vanilla yogurt**

**¼ cup orange juice**
**¼ cup cream sherry**
**Sprigs fresh mint, for garnish**

In the work bowl of a food processor or the container of a blender, puree the peaches with the lemon juice and sugar. Add the yogurt, orange juice, and sherry; process until pureed. Chill overnight. Serve in small bowls or wine goblets, garnished with a sprig of fresh mint.

# MEXICAN TORTILLA SOUP

## SERVES 6

1 tablespoon olive oil, or as needed
2 large onions, peeled and chopped
3 large tomatoes, finely chopped
8 to 10 cups chicken stock
1 can (4 ounces) chopped green chiles
1 bay leaf
1 teaspoon chopped cilantro
1 teaspoon chopped fresh basil

1 teaspoon minced garlic
½ cup vegetable oil
7 or 8 corn tortillas, cut into ½-inch strips
Salt, to taste
1 ripe avocado, peeled and sliced, for garnish
½ cup sour cream, for accompaniment
½ pound Monterey jack cheese, grated

In a large skillet over medium heat, warm the olive oil. Add the onion and saute until limp. Add the tomato and saute until it softens and browns a bit. Remove from the heat and set aside.

Meanwhile, in a large saucepan over low heat, simmer the stock. Add the chiles, bay leaf, cilantro, basil, garlic, and reserved onion-tomato mixture. Return to a simmer and cook for at least 1 hour.

Place the skillet over medium-high heat. Warm the vegetable oil until hot, then fry the tortilla strips until crisp and golden. Drain on paper towel and salt lightly.

To serve, ladle the soup into 6 individual bowls. To each bowl add a handful of tortilla strips, 2 or 3 avocado slices, and a dollop of sour cream. Top with the grated cheese and serve immediately.

# COWBOY BLACK BEAN SOUP
## WITH
## JALAPENO CREAM

SERVES 4 TO 6

½ pound dried black beans
6 cups chicken or vegetable stock
8 cups water
1 can (28 ounces) tomatoes with juice,
   chopped

2½ teaspoons ground cumin
Salt and pepper, to taste
½ cup chopped Walla Walla sweet onion or
   red Bermuda onion, for garnish
Chopped cilantro, for garnish

JALAPENO CREAM

1 cup sour cream
2 pickled jalapeno peppers, minced

3 tablespoons chopped cilantro

Soak the beans in cold water to cover for 1 hour. Drain. In a Dutch oven or stockpot over high heat, combine the beans, stock, and the water. Bring to a boil, stirring occasionally, then reduce the heat and simmer uncovered for about 1 hour.

Stir in the tomatoes with their juice and the cumin. Cook until the beans are soft (about 1½ hours). Remove from the heat and let cool for 15 minutes.

In the container of a blender or the work bowl of a food processor, puree the beans in

batches until smooth, then return the beans to the pot. Bring the soup to a simmer and season with the salt and pepper.

Prepare the Jalapeno Cream. To serve, ladle the soup into individual bowls and add a heaping teaspoonful of Jalapeno Cream to each. Sprinkle with the chopped onion and cilantro.

*Jalapeno Cream:* In a small bowl whisk together the sour cream, jalapeno peppers, and cilantro.

# ALMOST WHITE CHILI

SERVES 8

½ pound dried navy beans
1 medium onion, peeled and chopped
2 cloves garlic, peeled and minced
4 cups chicken stock
2½ teaspoons ground cumin
2 teaspoons dried oregano
¼ teaspoon cayenne pepper
3 whole cloves, crushed
1 can (4 ounces) green chiles
2 pounds chicken breasts, cooked, skinned, and chopped

½ cup chopped celery
1 can (14½ ounces) Roma tomatoes with juice, chopped
Sour cream and salsa, for accompaniment
3 to 4 tablespoons chopped cilantro, for garnish
3 to 4 tablespoons chopped onion, for garnish

In a stockpot over medium heat, combine the beans, the 1 medium onion chopped, the garlic, and stock; reduce the heat and simmer until the beans are tender (about 3 hours).

Add the cumin, oregano, cayenne, cloves, chiles, chicken, celery, and tomatoes with their juice. Bring to a boil, then reduce the heat and simmer for 30 minutes. Ladle into individual bowls and top each with the sour cream, salsa, cilantro, and 3 to 4 tablespoons chopped onion.

# CHILI VERDE

SERVES 6 TO 8

I serve this ladled over bowls full of refried beans and garnished with sour cream, salsa, freshly grated Parmesan, and chopped cilantro. Large corn or flour tortillas serve as scoops. This is a superb dish for a crowd!

1 tablespoon butter
2 large chuck roasts (4 to 5 pounds total), trimmed and cubed
3 cloves garlic, peeled and minced
2 large onions, peeled and chopped
2 large cans (28 ounces each) stewed tomatoes

1 or 2 cans (16 ounces each) green chiles, or to taste
1 jar (12 ounces) salsa
2 teaspoons dried oregano
1 teaspoon sugar
½ to ¾ teaspoon ground cumin
Salt, to taste

In a large skillet over medium heat, warm the butter. Add the beef cubes and cook until browned. Add the garlic and onion; cook for 10 minutes. Add the remaining ingredients; bring to a boil, then reduce the heat and simmer, covered, for 3 to 4 hours, stirring occasionally. The chili will become thick like stew. Serve hot.

# Entrees

# FRESH GRILLED SALMON

## SERVES 4

4 to 6 pounds fresh king or silver salmon
2 tablespoons freshly grated Parmesan
 cheese

MARINADE

½ cup oil
½ cup red wine vinegar
½ teaspoon dried thyme
½ teaspoon dried oregano

2 tablespoons chopped parsley
2 tablespoons butter

½ teaspoon dried basil
1 clove garlic, peeled and minced
1 teaspoon soy sauce

Prepare the Marinade and place the salmon in it for 1 to 4 hours.

Prepare a barbecue. When the coals are hot, sprinkle each side of the marinated salmon with the Parmesan cheese and parsley. Dot with the butter. Fold a piece of aluminum

foil into a boat shape and cook the salmon inside the foil boat until tender and cooked through.

*Marinade:* Combine all the ingredients and mix well.

# SALMON WITH CREAMY MUSTARD SAUCE

### SERVES 4

1 cup plus 3 tablespoons whipping cream
1 cup dry white wine
½ cup dry vermouth
½ cup finely minced onion, such as Walla Walla sweet, Vidalia, or Texas sweet
4 salmon steaks (6 to 8 ounces each), 1 inch thick

4 tablespoons butter, melted
2 tablespoons Dijon mustard
⅛ cup chopped fresh chives
⅛ cup chopped parsley
Salt and pepper, to taste
4 sprigs parsley, for garnish

In a small bowl stiffly whip the 3 tablespoons whipping cream; set aside in the refrigerator. Meanwhile, in a large skillet over medium-high heat, combine the wine, vermouth, and onion. Bring to a boil and cook until the liquid is reduced by half (5 to 7 minutes). Add the remaining 1 cup whipping cream and bring to a boil again.

Reduce the heat to low. Add the salmon; cover and simmer until the fish is just cooked (about 10 minutes). Remove the fish from the skillet, place on a serving platter, and cover with aluminum foil to keep warm.

Increase the heat to high under the skillet and cook the fish liquid until it is reduced to 1 cup, stirring frequently. Reduce the heat to low and gradually add the melted butter; whisk until combined. Add the mustard, chives, and chopped parsley. Remove from the heat and fold in the chilled whipped cream. Season with the salt and pepper. Spoon the sauce over the warm fish and garnish with the sprigs of parsley.

---

### THE SKINNY ON SALMON

Chinook, or King, salmon is considered the best salmon to serve. It's the largest of the five types of salmon caught in the Pacific Northwest. The rich, buttery flesh, which ranges from deep red to white, separates into large chunks when cooked. Although for years the red-fleshed variety has been deemed superior to the white, there's no difference in flavor. Because of this belief, however, the lighter fleshed King salmon is sometimes lower in price. Take advantage of the savings; whether the salmon's flesh is deep red or pearly white, the flavor is extraordinary.

# SCALLOPS AND MUSHROOM PHYLLO BUNDLES

SERVES 8

Don't be intimidated by phyllo dough. Just remember to keep the unused portion under a damp kitchen towel so it won't dry out. It's well worth the little extra effort.

1 cup butter
1 pound mushrooms, sliced
1 cup dry white wine
10 ounces cream cheese, at room
   temperature

Salt and pepper, to taste
3 eggs, beaten
2½ pounds scallops, patted dry
16 sheets phyllo dough

ROUX

3 teaspoons butter

3 teaspoons flour

Prepare the Roux and keep warm. In a large skillet over medium heat, melt ¼ cup of the butter. Add the mushrooms and saute until tender. Remove the mushrooms from the skillet and set aside.

Add the wine to the skillet, increase the heat to high, and cook until the liquid is reduced by half. Reduce the heat to low; add the cream cheese and stir until melted, then bring the mixture to a gentle simmer. Gradually whisk in the Roux, blending until thickened and smooth. Season with the salt and pepper. Remove from the heat and let cool. Blend in the eggs, reserved mushrooms, and scallops.

Preheat the oven to 400°F. Butter a baking sheet or line it with parchment paper; set aside. In a small saucepan melt the remaining ¾ cup butter. Lay 1 sheet of phyllo on a smooth work surface. Brush with some of the

melted butter and top with a second sheet of phyllo. Spoon ⅛ of the scallop mixture in a strip along the short end of the phyllo dough, leaving a 2- to 3-inch margin at the scallop end, as well as a ½-inch margin on each side. Beginning with the scallop end, tightly roll up the phyllo, enclosing the scallops, until it's two-thirds rolled. Fold in the sides of the phyllo and brush the remaining third of the dough with some of the melted butter. Finish rolling the phyllo.

Place the roll seam side down on the prepared baking sheet and brush the top lightly with some of the melted butter. Repeat with the remaining phyllo and scallop mixture. Bake until golden (15 to 20 minutes).

*Roux:* In a small skillet over low heat, melt the butter. Gradually stir in the flour and cook, stirring, for at least 5 minutes.

# SEAFOOD AND BASIL RISOTTO

SERVES 6

This cookbook contains all my favorite dishes, but this is tops. It is a total "treat yourself to the best." The only thing that would make it better is to have someone cook it for you.

4 tablespoons butter
1 small onion, peeled and finely chopped
1½ cups uncooked Arborio rice (Italian short-grained rice)
5 cups chicken stock
⅓ cup whipping cream

8 to 10 ounces fresh crabmeat or shrimp or a combination of both
4 ounces goat cheese, such as Montrachet
⅓ cup chopped fresh basil or 1¼ tablespoons dried basil
Salt and pepper, to taste

In a large saucepan over medium heat, melt the butter. Add the onion and saute until limp (about 5 minutes). Add the rice and saute about 2 minutes. Add ½ cup of the stock; reduce the heat and simmer until the liquid is absorbed, stirring almost nonstop. Add the remaining stock in half-cup increments, stirring each time until the liquid is absorbed before adding more stock, until the rice is just tender but still firm to the bite and all the stock is absorbed into the rice (about 20 minutes).

Add the whipping cream and simmer for 2 minutes. Mix in the seafood, goat cheese, basil, and salt and pepper. Serve hot.

# CHICKEN BREASTS MEXICANA

SERVES 3 OR 4

I won my first cooking contest with this recipe and have very fond memories of testing, retesting, and persuading friends and neighbors to give their opinions of it. It's a nice twist on Mexican food and is a simple and lovely entree. Serve it with a halved and hollowed-out red or yellow bell pepper, one half filled with salsa, the other with guacamole. Accompany it with refried beans and Mexican rice.

3 whole chicken breasts, halved, boned, and skinned
4 tablespoons butter
¼ teaspoon ground cumin

¼ teaspoon chili powder
1½ cups "nacho cheese" tortilla chips, finely crushed

FILLING

8 ounces cream cheese, at room temperature
½ cup freshly grated sharp Cheddar cheese

1 can (4½ ounces) green chiles, diced
1 can (2½ ounces) black olives, chopped
3 tablespoons finely chopped onion

Preheat the oven to 350°F. Prepare the Filling and chill.

Pound the chicken breasts to ¼ inch thick; spread the Filling onto each breast. Roll up and secure the ends and seam with toothpicks.

In a medium skillet over medium heat, melt the butter. Add the cumin and chili powder; stir to blend. Roll the chicken breasts in this mixture, then in the crushed tortilla chips. Bake until the chicken is no longer pink near the bone (about 25 minutes).

*Filling:* Combine all the ingredients and mix well.

# CHICKEN WITH ARTICHOKES AND MUSHROOMS

### SERVES 4 TO 6

This is a fine dish to serve to guests; you can prepare it ahead of time and bake it just before serving. It's as simple or as elegant as the side dishes you choose to serve with it. A wild rice blend and Baby Dilled Carrots are good companions. Try Angela Pia for a terrific finale.

**3 pounds chicken breasts and thighs**
**2 teaspoons salt**
**½ teaspoon ground black pepper**
**½ teaspoon paprika**
**8 tablespoons butter**

**3 cups marinated artichoke hearts**
**½ pound mushrooms, thickly sliced**
**2½ tablespoons flour**
**1 cup chicken stock**
**⅓ cup dry sherry**

Preheat the oven to 350°F. Sprinkle the chicken with the salt, pepper, and paprika. In a large skillet over medium heat, melt 4 tablespoons of the butter. Add the chicken and cook until browned on the outside and no longer pink on the inside. Transfer the chicken to a casserole dish and top with the artichoke hearts.

Melt the remaining 4 tablespoons butter in the skillet. Add the mushrooms and saute over medium heat until limp. Sprinkle with the flour, then add the stock and sherry and simmer until the sauce is thickened (5 to 7 minutes). Pour the sauce over the chicken in the casserole, cover, and bake for 1½ hours.

# GRILLED CHICKEN WITH BLUEBERRY MUSTARD SAUCE

SERVES 4

I laugh when I think of the first time I served this dish. I had just welcomed some guests who were proceeding to tell me how dreadful their vacation had started out. They had purchased box seats to a sporting event only to find out they had been booked for the wrong night. The next evening the bed and breakfast where they had planned to stay had overbooked and didn't have a room for them. As they were telling me all this, it dawned on me that I had promised to cook them dinner and had completely forgotten! Now, you must understand that when I do dinners, I usually cook all day. It was already 6:30 P.M.! A look of shock passed over my face and they guessed what had happened. Luckily they were good sports and had all evening to wait. They swam while I cooked and raced around like a madwoman. This dish was the result of having ripe blueberries on our bushes. Serve it with Coconut Rice and you've got a winning meal! They loved it; I hope you do too.

4 tablespoons lemon juice
3 tablespoons olive oil
4 chicken breasts, boned and skinned
1 cup finely chopped onion
2 teaspoons dry mustard
2½ tablespoons Dijon mustard
2 tablespoons honey

4 tablespoons dry white wine, or more to taste
2 cups fresh or frozen blueberries
¼ teaspoon ground cinnamon
½ cup whipping cream
Fresh blueberries, for garnish (optional)

In a large bowl combine 2 tablespoons each of the lemon juice and olive oil. Add the chicken and let marinate for a few hours.

To make the sauce, in a large saucepan over medium heat, warm the remaining 1 tablespoon olive oil. Add the onion and saute until soft. Add the dry mustard, the remaining 2 tablespoons lemon juice, the Dijon mustard, honey, wine, the blueberries, and cinnamon. Bring to a boil, then reduce the heat and cook for 10 minutes. Remove from the heat and let cool slightly, then pour the mixture into the work bowl of a food processor and process until all the berries are crushed but not pureed. The mixture should still be fairly chunky.

Return the mixture to the saucepan over low heat, add the whipping cream, and simmer until the sauce is thick. For a thinner sauce, add 2 to 4 tablespoons more wine.

While the sauce is cooking, grill the marinated chicken over medium coals until springy (about 5 minutes per side), basting occasionally with the marinade. To serve, pool some sauce on a small portion of the plate and top with a chicken breast. Drizzle more sauce over the chicken and garnish with a few fresh blueberries, if desired.

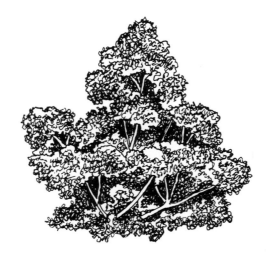

# LEMON AND BLUE CHEESE CHICKEN

## SERVES 6

⅔ cup sour cream
3 ounces (about a heaping ½ cup) Oregon
  blue cheese
2½ tablespoons freshly squeezed lemon
  juice
1 tablespoon sliced green onion
2 teaspoons freshly grated lemon zest

¾ cup flour
1 teaspoon salt
1¾ teaspoons dried rosemary, crumbled
¾ teaspoon freshly ground black pepper
6 chicken breasts
⅓ cup butter

Preheat the oven to 350°F. In a small bowl combine the sour cream, blue cheese, lemon juice, green onion, and lemon zest; set aside. In a shallow dish combine the flour, salt, rosemary, and ground pepper. Add the chicken and turn to coat each piece.

In a large skillet over medium-high heat, melt the butter. Add the coated chicken and saute until golden. Transfer the chicken to a greased baking dish and arrange skin side up. Spread the reserved sour cream mixture over the chicken. Bake until the mixture is nicely browned and the chicken is cooked through (35 to 40 minutes).

# CITRUS AND HONEY PORK TENDERLOIN

### SERVES 6 TO 8

1½ tablespoons freshly grated orange zest
2 tablespoons minced fresh lemon thyme
   or 1 tablespoon dried thyme, crumbled
1 teaspoon freshly ground black pepper
4 cloves garlic, peeled and minced
2 pork tenderloins, 10 to 12 ounces each

¾ cup freshly squeezed orange juice
1 tablespoon soy sauce
2 tablespoons rice vinegar
4¼ tablespoons olive oil
6 tablespoons honey

In a small bowl make a paste of the orange zest, thyme, ground pepper, and garlic. Rub the paste into the pork, then place the pork in a large bowl.

In another small bowl combine the orange juice, soy sauce, vinegar, and olive oil; pour it over the pork and let marinate at least 4 hours. (I find it only gets better the longer you can let it rest.)

Preheat the oven to 425°F. Place the pork in a baking pan or an ovenproof skillet. Drizzle with 3 tablespoons of the honey. Roast the pork for 15 minutes, then turn. Spoon any pan juices over the pork, then drizzle with the remaining 3 tablespoons honey. Roast for another 15 minutes for medium-cooked pork, basting again at least twice with the pan juices.

Remove the pork from the oven and let stand for about 5 minutes. Carve into ¼-inch-thick slices.

---

*I saw him go the way of all flesh, that is to say towards the kitchen.*
   —John Webster (c. 1580–1625)

# PORK CHOP AND APPLESAUCE CASSEROLE

SERVES 3 OR 4

As this dish cooks, the apples bake down and become applesauce. The pork is permeated with the onion-apple flavor, and it's delicious. It also makes your kitchen smell like heaven.

6 to 8 pork chops
6 to 8 tart apples, such as Granny Smith, peeled, cored, and sliced
1 tablespoon ground cinnamon
½ cup sugar

1 large onion, peeled and thinly sliced
1 tablespoon garlic salt
3 tablespoons chopped parsley
Salt and pepper, to taste

Preheat the broiler; broil the chops for 5 minutes. Remove and keep warm.

Preheat the oven to 400°F. Place the apples in the bottom of a buttered 13- by 9-inch casserole dish. Sprinkle with the cinnamon and sugar, then top with the sliced onion. Arrange the pork chops over all and sprinkle with the garlic salt, parsley, and salt and pepper. Cover with aluminum foil and bake for 1 to 1½ hours.

# STUFFED PORK CHOPS WITH APPLE CIDER SAUCE

SERVES 4

4 rib pork chops, 1 inch thick
1 clove garlic, peeled and split
½ cup chicken stock
1¾ cups apple juice

DRESSING

1 tablespoon butter
¼ cup chopped onion
1 clove garlic, peeled and minced
½ cup chopped celery
½ cup sliced mushrooms
2 teaspoons chopped fresh sage
1 cup bread crumbs

½ cup whipping cream
1 teaspoon chopped fresh basil
1 teaspoon chopped fresh summer savory
Salt and pepper, to taste

2 tablespoons chopped parsley
¼ teaspoon salt
¼ teaspoon paprika
Dash freshly ground black pepper
1 egg, beaten
Milk, to bind dressing

Preheat the oven to 350°F. Trim the chops of fat, then rub with the garlic. Cut a large gash in the side of each chop. Prepare the Dressing, then spoon it into the gash in each chop and fasten with several toothpicks.

In the same skillet used to prepare the Dressing, sear the stuffed chops on both sides over high heat. Add the stock and ¾ cup of the apple juice to the skillet and place it in the oven. Cover and bake for 50 to 60 minutes.

Remove the chops and keep warm on a plate in a warm oven. Strain the remaining liquid in the skillet through cheesecloth and set aside. Deglaze the skillet over high heat with the remaining 1 cup apple juice, scraping up any browned bits. Return the strained skillet liquid to the pan and add the whipping cream. Bring to a low boil and whisk until the mixture is reduced and thick, then cook until the sauce coats the back of a spoon (about 10 minutes longer). Whisk in the juices from the plate holding the pork chops, then add the basil, savory, and salt and pepper. Pour the mixture over the chops and serve.

*Dressing:* In a large ovenproof skillet over low heat, melt the butter. Add the onion, garlic, celery, and mushrooms; saute for 10 minutes. Transfer to a large bowl and add the remaining ingredients, using enough milk to moisten so that the mixture holds together.

# ELLENSBURG LAMB WITH ROSEMARY MUSTARD

## SERVES 2 TO 4

There's always a few in the crowd who feel that New Zealand lamb is the best. I'm not so sure. Not only is Ellensburg just a hop, skip, and a jump from us (and that translates as fresh), but their lamb is usually more tender. Do a taste test for yourself sometime. Here at the inn we do taste tests frequently—not just with meats but also with vanilla ice cream, nonalcoholic beer, Dijon mustard, breakfast sausage, and more. I keep hoping that *Consumer Reports*' Ralph Nader will ask me to join his taste team. Talk about a dream job . . .

⅓ cup coarse-grained prepared mustard
⅓ cup Madeira wine
2½ tablespoons dried rosemary, crushed
3 cloves garlic, peeled and finely minced

2 teaspoons freshly cracked black peppercorns
1 Ellensburg tenderloin of lamb

In a small bowl combine the mustard, Maderia, rosemary, garlic, and cracked peppercorns. Rub the mixture into the lamb, cover, and chill overnight.

Preheat the oven to 400°F. Roast the lamb on the rack of a roasting pan in the middle of the oven until a meat thermometer registers 140°F for medium rare (20 to 25 minutes). Remove the lamb from the oven and place on a cutting board; let stand for 6 to 8 minutes before slicing.

# $\mathcal{H}$ERBED LAMB CHOPS
## WITH
## APPLE MINT CHUTNEY

### SERVES 4

8 loin lamb chops, 1½ inches thick

MARINADE

4 tablespoons freshly squeezed lemon juice
2 tablespoons honey mustard
3 tablespoons honey
3 tablespoons red wine vinegar
2½ teaspoons dried oregano

APPLE-MINT CHUTNEY

1 cup raisins
1 large tart apple, such as Granny Smith or
  McIntosh, peeled, cored, and cut into
  large dice

Fresh mint sprigs, for garnish

1½ teaspoons dried rosemary, crushed
3 cloves garlic, peeled and crushed
⅓ cup olive oil
1 teaspoon soy sauce

½ cup chopped fresh mint
2 tablespoons freshly squeezed lemon juice
1 teaspoon mint jelly
1 teaspoon honey

Prepare the Marinade. Place the chops in a shallow baking dish and pour the Marinade over top; turn to coat both sides. Chill overnight if possible; if cooking the same day, let the chops marinate at room temperature for at least 2 to 3 hours, turning occasionally.

Preheat the broiler. Arrange the marinated chops on the broiler pan and broil about 4 minutes per side for medium rare. Transfer the chops to a serving platter. Garnish with the mint, and serve with the Apple-Mint Chutney.

*Marinade:* Combine all the ingredients in a bowl and whisk together.

*Apple-Mint Chutney:* Soak the raisins in just enough water to cover until soft (at least 20 minutes). Drain; reserve the liquid. Place all the ingredients except the raisin liquid in the work bowl of a food processor; blend well. Add the liquid a little at a time if the chutney is too dry. This mixture should be chunky.

# BEEF FILETS WITH ROQUEFORT BUTTER

SERVES 4

**4 beef filets, about 6 ounces each**

MARINADE

**2 tablespoons juniper berries, crushed**
**1 teaspoon freshly ground black pepper**
**⅓ cup Pinot Noir**

**¼ cup olive oil**
**⅓ cup finely chopped parsley**

ROQUEFORT BUTTER

**4 tablespoons butter**
**1 teaspoon minced garlic**
**¼ cup crumbled Roquefort cheese**

**1 teaspoon chopped parsley**
**¼ teaspoon freshly ground black pepper**

SAUCE

**2 cups beef stock**
**3 tablespoons butter**

**1 tablespoon minced shallot**
**2 cups Pinot Noir**

Prepare the Marinade. Place the beef filets in a large baking dish, pour the Marinade over top, and let stand for 4 hours.

Prepare the Roquefort Butter and the Sauce. Grill the steaks over hot coals to the desired degree of doneness. Transfer to individual serving plates. Top each filet with a dollop of Roquefort Butter and spoon the Sauce around the meat.

*Marinade:* Combine all the ingredients and mix well.

*Roquefort Butter:* Combine all the ingredients in a bowl and mix well. Chill.

*Sauce:* In a medium saucepan over medium-high heat, cook the stock until it is reduced by half; set aside. In a medium skillet over medium heat, melt 1 tablespoon of the butter. Add the shallot and saute until soft. Add the wine and cook until the liquid is reduced by half. Add the reduced stock and continue to reduce until the sauce coats the back of a spoon. Beat in the remaining 2 tablespoons butter.

# SPICY KAL-BI RIBS

### SERVES 6 TO 8

6 pounds beef short ribs, cut into ¾-inch
  strips
4½ cups water
1¾ cups soy sauce
1¼ cups sugar
12 cloves garlic, peeled and minced

6 green onions, chopped
4 tablespoons sesame seeds
4 tablespoons sesame oil
4½ tablespoons chopped fresh ginger
2½ tablespoons honey
4 teaspoons Tabasco Sauce

Arrange the beef in a roasting pan. In a large bowl combine all the remaining ingredients; blend well. Pour over the beef, cover, and marinate for at least 24 hours.

Broil the marinated beef over hot coals or in the broiler, turning once and cooking to your taste.

---

### A BIT ON BEEF

When a recipe such as Spicy Kal-bi Ribs calls for thin slices of beef, simplify the slicing by placing the meat you'll be using in the freezer until it's partially frozen (about 1 hour). This makes the meat much firmer and easier to slice. For the most tenderness, cut across the grain.

---

# EGGPLANT PARMIGIANA

SERVES 4 TO 6

1 medium eggplant (1½ pounds)
½ cup bread crumbs
¾ cup freshly grated Parmesan cheese

¼ cup mayonnaise
8 ounces mozzarella cheese, thinly sliced

TOMATO BASIL SAUCE
Makes 3½ cups

2 cans (6 ounces each) tomato paste
3 cans (6 ounces each) water
2¼ teaspoons chopped fresh basil or
    1 teaspoons dried basil, crushed
1½ teaspoons dried oregano

1 tablespoon brown sugar
½ teaspoon salt
½ teaspoon ground black pepper
1 clove garlic, peeled and minced

Preheat the oven to 425°F. Prepare the Tomato Basil Sauce and set aside.

Wash and trim the eggplant, then cut into ½-inch slices. On a piece of waxed paper or a large plate, combine the bread crumbs and ¼ cup of the Parmesan.

Spread the mayonnaise thinly on each slice of eggplant, then dip both sides of the coated slices into the crumb mixture. Place them on an ungreased baking sheet and bake until the eggplant is fork-tender (about 15 minutes). Remove from the oven; lower the heat to 375°F.

In a greased baking dish, arrange the cooked eggplant slices in 2 lines with each slice slightly overlapping the next. Spread each slice with a small amount of the Tomato Basil Sauce; cover with the mozzarella and sprinkle with the remaining ½ cup Parmesan. Bake until the cheese is melted (about 20 minutes).

*Tomato Basil Sauce:* In a large saucepan over medium heat, combine all the ingredients. Simmer for 15 minutes. Refrigerate any leftovers.

## A PRIMER ON PARMESAN

When I mention Parmesan cheese anywhere in this book, I am not referring to that canned, salty, dry, orange powder you can find on the shelves at grocery stores. Authentic Parmesan cheese is with the specialty cheeses in the deli case. This wonderful creation has a sharp flavor and crumbly texture. It's cut into wedges and is usually labeled Parmigiano-Reggiano. This is the region in Italy where Parmesan cheese originated. I use it liberally. When serving pasta, always have a bowl of freshly grated Parmesan on the table.

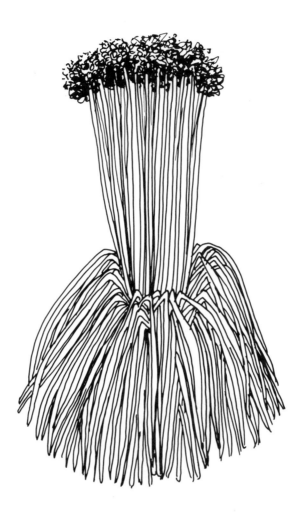

# Vegetables

# ASPARAGUS WITH HAZELNUT LEMON SAUCE

SERVES 4

8 tablespoons butter
¾ cup chopped hazelnuts
Freshly grated zest of 1 large lemon
2½ tablespoons freshly squeezed lemon
    juice

1 pound fresh asparagus, rinsed, tough
    stem ends removed
Salt and pepper, to taste

In a large skillet over medium heat, melt the butter. Add the nuts and toss until slightly browned (4 to 5 minutes). Add the lemon zest and juice; stir to blend, then remove from the heat and keep warm.

In a vegetable steamer over boiling water, steam the asparagus until tender but firm when pierced with a fork. Place on a serving platter and season with the salt and pepper. Pour the hot lemon butter sauce over top.

---

### A TIP ON ASPARAGUS

Before you cook asparagus, break off the woody ends of the stalks. Mother Nature makes this very easy. Grasp the stem of the asparagus in one hand and the tip in the other. Gently bend the tip. The stalk should break where the asparagus is still tender. You can save the tough stems and freeze them; they make a good stock base for cream of asparagus soup.

---

# ABY DILLED CARROTS

SERVES 4

1 pound baby carrots, scraped
3 tablespoons butter

1 tablespoon chopped fresh dill or
   1 teaspoon dried dill weed
Salt and pepper, to taste

In a vegetable steamer over boiling water, steam the carrots until tender but still crisp. Remove from the steamer, drain, and set aside.

In a large saucepan over medium heat, melt the butter. Add the dill and steamed carrots. Toss gently, then season with the salt and pepper.

# SOPHISTICATED CARROT SOUFFLE

### SERVES 4 TO 6

Butter, for dish
1 pound carrots, scraped and cut into
    pieces
4 eggs
¾ cup flour
⅛ teaspoon salt
1 teaspoon baking powder

½ cup sugar
1 tablespoon butter, softened
2 teaspoons vanilla extract
1 teaspoon ground nutmeg
2 to 3 tablespoons freshly grated orange
    zest

Preheat the oven to 350°F. Butter a souffle dish and set aside.

In a large saucepan over medium-high heat, boil the carrots in just enough water to cover until tender. Remove from the heat and drain. Transfer to a large bowl; mash, then whip until smooth. Let cool to room temperature. Add the eggs one at a time, beating for 1 minute after each addition.

Sift together the flour, salt, and baking powder. Blend into the carrot mixture along with the sugar, butter, vanilla, nutmeg, and zest. Pour the mixture into the prepared souffle dish and bake until puffed and firm (about 40 minutes).

# BROCCOLI LEMON MOUSSE
## WITH
## LEMON CREAM SAUCE

### SERVES 4 TO 6

2 pounds fresh broccoli
¼ cup whipping cream or half-and-half
1 egg
Freshly grated zest and juice of 1 small
  lemon

Salt and pepper, to taste
Butter, for dish
Lemon slices, for garnish

LEMON CREAM SAUCE

2 tablespoons freshly squeezed lemon juice
2½ tablespoons whipping cream

1 cup butter, very cold and cut into cubes
Salt and freshly ground pepper, to taste

Cut the broccoli florets from the stems.
Trim and peel the stems, then slice
thinly. Steam or boil the florets and stems
until tender but still crisp. Drain, then place
the broccoli on paper towels and blot dry.
Reserve a few florets for garnish.

Puree the prepared broccoli in the work bowl
of a food processor until smooth. Transfer to
a large bowl and beat in the cream, egg, and
lemon zest and juice. Season with the salt
and pepper.

Preheat the oven to 350°F. Butter a large
souffle dish or 4 to 6 small ramekins. Transfer
the broccoli mixture to the prepared dish.
Place in a roasting pan and pour in enough
hot water to come at least halfway up the

sides of the dish. Bake until firm (40 to 45
minutes). Remove from the water and let
cool in the dish for 15 minutes. Meanwhile,
prepare the Lemon Cream Sauce.

To serve, unmold the mousse onto a serving
platter or individual plates. Top with the
Lemon Cream Sauce, then garnish with the
reserved broccoli florets and the lemon slices.
Pass the remaining sauce separately.

*Lemon Cream Sauce:* In a small saucepan over
medium-high heat, boil the lemon juice until
it's reduced to a glaze. Remove from the heat
and whisk in the cream, then slowly whisk in
the butter, a small amount at a time. Cook
until the mixture is reduced by one-fourth.
Season with the salt and pepper.

# BROCCOLI WITH BASIL ORANGE SAUCE

### SERVES 4

**1 pound fresh broccoli spears, tough stem ends removed**

BASIL ORANGE SAUCE

**⅓ cup plus 2 tablespoons water**
**⅓ cup freshly squeezed orange juice**
**1½ tablespoons chopped fresh basil**

**Orange slices, for garnish**

**1½ teaspoons freshly grated orange zest**
**¼ teaspoon salt**
**2 teaspoons cornstarch**

Prepare the Basil Orange Sauce; keep warm.

Arrange the broccoli spears in a vegetable steamer over boiling water. Steam until tender but still crisp. Remove from the heat. Pour the Basil Orange Sauce over the broccoli. Garnish with the orange slices.

*Basil Orange Sauce:* In a medium saucepan over medium heat, combine the ⅓ cup water, the orange juice, basil, orange zest, and salt. Bring to a boil. Combine the remaining 2 tablespoons water with the cornstarch; stir well until dissolved, then slowly add to the orange juice mixture, stirring constantly to avoid lumps. Cook until the sauce is thickened and shiny.

#  FRESH GREEN BEANS WITH MINT

## SERVES 4 TO 6

Mint grows wild in our yard at the inn. We have apple mint, lemon mint, spearmint, peppermint, pineapple mint, and some mints I can't even identify. Mint is not only good for tea, but you can add it to vegetables, green salads, fruit salads, and soups, and it makes a pungent garnish.

Find a shady spot and plant some for yourself. You'll soon have enough to supply the whole neighborhood, and you'll find out what a pleasure it is to have around the kitchen.

**1 pound fresh green beans, ends trimmed, beans cut in half diagonally**
**6 tablespoons olive oil**
**1 clove garlic, peeled and minced**

**¼ cup chopped fresh mint or 1 tablespoon dried mint**
**Salt and pepper, to taste**

Steam the beans in a vegetable steamer over boiling water until tender but still crisp (6 to 8 minutes). Remove from the heat and drain.

Meanwhile, in a large skillet over medium heat, warm the oil. Add the garlic and saute until golden but not browned. Stir in the drained beans, mint, and salt and pepper.

# GREEN BEANS IN HOT VINAIGRETTE

### SERVES 4

1 pound fresh green beans, ends trimmed
3 tablespoons olive oil
½ cup thinly sliced green onion
2 tablespoons chopped parsley
1 clove garlic, peeled and minced

1 tablespoon rice wine vinegar
1 teaspoon raspberry mustard or Dijon
  mustard
Salt and pepper, to taste

In a vegetable steamer over boiling water, steam the beans until tender but still crisp. Remove from the heat and drain.

In a large skillet over medium heat, warm the oil. Add the green onion, parsley, garlic, vinegar, and mustard; whisk until well combined. Add the drained beans and toss until the beans are well coated. Add the salt and pepper; serve hot.

# GRANDMA SOPHIE'S SWEET AND SOUR CABBAGE

### SERVES 6 TO 8

**4 thin slices bacon**
**3 pounds red cabbage, finely shredded**
**2 large apples, peeled, cored, and chopped**
**2 tablespoons brown sugar**

**⅓ cup cider vinegar**
**½ cup dry white wine**
**1 cup water**

In a large skillet over medium heat, fry the bacon until almost crisp. With a slotted spoon, remove it from the pan and place on paper towels to drain. When cool, crumble and set aside.

Add the cabbage to the bacon drippings in the pan and stir until the cabbage is wilted. Add the apples, brown sugar, vinegar, wine, and the water. Bring to a boil, then reduce the heat and simmer until the cabbage is tender (30 to 45 minutes). Stir in the crumbled bacon and serve.

# HERBED CHERRY TOMATOES

### SERVES 4

You can use just about any combination of herbs in this recipe. Basil, Greek oregano, chives, and lemon thyme are what I use most of the time, since they are right outside my kitchen door.

3 tablespoons butter
2 tablespoons olive oil
2 cloves garlic, peeled and minced
1 pint cherry tomatoes, stemmed

⅓ cup chopped fresh herbs
Salt and freshly ground black pepper, to taste

In a large skillet over medium heat, warm the butter and olive oil. Add the garlic and saute for about 1 minute. Add the tomatoes, fresh herbs, and salt and pepper; shake the pan to coat the tomatoes. Cook for 4 to 5 minutes, stirring or shaking the pan from time to time. Don't overcook or the tomato skins will split.

# ONEY GLAZED ONIONS

SERVES 4 TO 6

1½ pounds small whole cooking onions
5 tablespoons honey
3 tablespoons butter

½ teaspoon salt
¼ teaspoon freshly ground black pepper
⅓ cup dry sherry

Cut the tip ends off the unpeeled onions and cook them in boiling salted water just until tender (about 20 minutes). Drain, let cool, then slip off the skins.

In a large skillet over medium heat, combine the remaining ingredients. Stir well to blend.

Add the skinned onions; cover and cook until they are well glazed and tender (about 30 minutes), shaking the pan occasionally to prevent scorching. Uncover and cook until the onions turn golden brown (5 to 10 minutes longer).

# WALLA WALLA SWEET ONION SOUFFLES

## SERVES 4

4 large Walla Walla sweet onions
2 tablespoons balsamic vinegar
2 teaspoons sugar
2 tablespoons butter
2 tablespoons flour
¾ cup milk

½ cup freshly grated Romano cheese
¼ teaspoon dried oregano
¼ teaspoon dried basil
2 large eggs
¾ teaspoon salt
¼ teaspoon ground black pepper

Preheat the oven to 350°F. Peel the onions and cut them in half horizontally. Trim the bottoms if needed to make the onions sit flat. Place the onions, cut side up, in a 13- by 9-inch pan. Spoon the vinegar and sugar over each. Cover with aluminum foil and bake until tender when pierced with a fork (about 1 hour). Let cool.

Pull the centers from the onions, leaving ⅛ inch of the shell. Place the onion centers in a chopping bowl; set the shells aside. Reserve the pan liquid.

Finely chop the onion centers. In a Dutch oven or 3- to 4-quart pan over medium heat, melt the butter. Add the chopped onion centers and saute until limp. Add the flour and stir to create a roux. Whisk in the milk and reserved pan liquid; stir until the sauce thickens. Remove from the heat and blend in the cheese, oregano, and basil.

Transfer a little of the cheese sauce to a small bowl. Add the egg yolks one at a time, beating after each addition. (This will heat up the yolks without cooking them, as you would do if you just dropped them into the hot sauce.) Now add the egg yolk mixture to the sauce in the larger pan.

Whip the egg whites until they form stiff peaks. Carefully fold the egg whites, a little at a time, into the sauce.

Increase the oven temperature to 375°F. Gently fill the onion shells with the cheese mixture. Bake, uncovered, until the souffles are golden brown and puffed (25 to 30 minutes). Transfer the filled shells to plates. Season with the salt and pepper.

# SACRAMENTO SWEET POTATO CASSEROLE

### SERVES 6 TO 8

This dish calls for sweet potatoes, but I prefer to use yams. At a taste test I once held, I found that sweet potatoes seemed dry and starchy compared to yams. You decide. This dish is wonderful with either one.

4 to 6 sweet potatoes or yams, peeled and sliced
1 cup granulated sugar

½ cup butter
1 teaspoon vanilla extract
2 eggs

TOPPING

1 cup chopped pecans or walnuts
⅓ cup butter

⅓ cup flour
1 cup packed brown sugar

Boil the potatoes until tender, then whip with the granulated sugar, ½ cup butter, vanilla, and eggs. Place in a large casserole dish.

Preheat the oven to 350°F. Prepare the Topping. Crumble it on top of the potatoes

and bake until heated through (about 35 minutes).

*Topping:* Combine all the ingredients; mix well.

# $\mathscr{T}$HE FAMILY'S FAVORITE CORN

### SERVES 6 TO 8

This dish has been traditional at my family's holiday functions for years. When Dale and I were first married, I made this for one of his family's huge Swedish gatherings. I was feeling a little out of my element, as they were serving such traditional Swedish fare as potato sausage, *lefsa,* pickled herring, and cardamom bread. Luckily, this thoroughly American dish was a tremendous hit. Nowadays bringing a dish to either family gathering is easy: everyone just tells me to "bring the corn!"

2 packages (10 ounces each) frozen corn
  kernels
1 cup whipping cream
1 cup milk
1 teaspoon salt

¼ teaspoon MSG (optional)
6 teaspoons sugar
⅛ teaspoon ground white pepper
2 tablespoons butter
2 tablespoons flour

In a large saucepan over medium-high heat, combine the corn, cream, milk, salt, MSG (if used), sugar, and ground pepper. Bring to a boil, then reduce the heat and simmer for 5 minutes. Remove from the heat and set aside.

In a small saucepan over low heat, melt the butter. Sprinkle with the flour and stir continually for at least 5 minutes to form a roux. Add the roux a little at a time to the corn mixture, whisking to blend completely. Stir until thick. Serve hot.

# Potatoes
# and
# Rice

❖

# BABY RED-SKINNED POTATOES
## WITH
## GARLIC AND ROSEMARY

SERVES 4 TO 6

18 to 20 baby red-skinned potatoes (about 1½ pounds)
1 tablespoon butter
3 tablespoons olive oil
1 clove garlic, peeled and minced

1 teaspoon dried rosemary, crushed
½ teaspoon salt
¼ teaspoon freshly ground black pepper
3 tablespoons chopped parsley

Place the potatoes in a vegetable steamer over boiling water and cook until tender when pierced. Remove from the heat and set aside.

In a large skillet over medium heat, warm the butter and olive oil. Add the garlic and saute but don't let it brown, as this makes it bitter. Add the reserved potatoes, rosemary, salt, and ground pepper; toss gently. Top with the chopped parsley.

# ASHMERE ALL-PURPOSE POTATOES

### SERVES 3 TO 4

We serve these as a side dish for entrees at breakfast, but they are also a delicious fat-free alternative to French fries. You can cook Idaho russets or white- or red-skinned potatoes this way, but my favorite potato for this dish is the red skinned.

**Vegetable oil or nonstick spray, for baking sheet**

**3 large potatoes, peeled and sliced ⅛ inch thick**
**Seasoned salt, to taste**

Preheat the oven to 450°F. Oil a baking sheet and arrange the potato slices on it. Sprinkle with the seasoned salt and bake until golden.

To shorten the cooking time in the oven (as I do when serving these potatoes for breakfast), place the sliced potatoes on a microwavable plate. Sprinkle them with water, cover with plastic wrap, and microwave for 6 minutes and 15 seconds. Remove from the microwave, sprinkle with seasoned salt, place on an oiled baking sheet, and bake in a preheated 450°F oven for 5 to 6 minutes.

# COMPANY'S COMING STUFFED BAKED POTATOES

## SERVES 4

2 large baking potatoes
4 slices bacon
2 tablespoons butter
½ cup sour cream

4 tablespoons freshly grated Parmesan
   cheese
2 tablespoons minced green onion
Salt and pepper, to taste

Preheat the oven to 425°F. Bake the potatoes until easily pierced (about 45 minutes). Remove from the oven and reduce the heat to 350°F. Cut each potato in half lengthwise. Very gently scoop out the pulp into a medium bowl or the work bowl of a food processor; reserve the potato skins.

In a medium skillet over medium heat, fry the bacon until crisp. Drain on a paper towel. Let cool, then crumble and set aside.

To the potatoes in the bowl, add the butter and sour cream; whip until smooth. Add 2 tablespoons of the Parmesan cheese, the crumbled bacon, green onion, and salt and pepper. Stir until well combined.

Fill the reserved potato skins with the mashed potato mixture. (For an elegant look, use a pastry bag and pipe this mixture into the potato skins.) Sprinkle the potatoes with the remaining 2 tablespoons Parmesan cheese and bake until they're slightly golden and heated through (15 to 20 minutes).

# HERBED POTATO PUFFS

SERVES 6 TO 8

2 cups mashed potatoes, seasoned and
  chilled
4 eggs, beaten
3½ tablespoons flour
2½ tablespoons chopped fresh chives
½ teaspoon dried basil
1¼ tablespoons baking powder

1 clove garlic, peeled and minced
1 teaspoon onion powder
1 teaspoon salt
½ teaspoon ground black pepper
1 to 2 cups vegetable oil
Sour cream, for accompaniment
Applesauce, for accompaniment

In a large bowl combine the potatoes, eggs, flour, chives, basil, baking powder, garlic, onion powder, salt, and pepper. In a large, heavy skillet over medium heat, warm the oil. Drop heaping tablespoons of the potato mixture into the hot oil and cook until golden brown on each side. Remove from the oil and drain on paper towels. Serve immediately with the sour cream and applesauce on the side.

# CREAMY RISOTTO

SERVES 4 TO 6

The keys to successful risotto are: you must use Arborio rice (Italian short-grained rice); you shouldn't add too much liquid all at once; and you must stir the rice continuously as it cooks.

**6 cups chicken stock**
**8 tablespoons butter**
**1 medium onion, peeled and finely**
  **chopped**

**2 cups Arborio rice**
**6 tablespoons freshly grated Parmesan**
  **cheese**
**Freshly ground black pepper, to taste**

In a large saucepan over medium-high heat, bring the stock to a boil; cover and keep warm. In a large soup kettle over medium heat, melt 4 tablespoons of the butter. Add the onion and saute until limp. Stir in the rice and saute until translucent and coated with butter (1 to 2 minutes). Add ½ cup of the hot stock and simmer until the liquid is completely absorbed (about 1 minute), stirring constantly. Repeat with the remaining stock, adding only ½ cup at a time and stirring continuously. You'll do this for 20 to 25 minutes. (It's worth the effort!)

When all the liquid is absorbed, the rice should be creamy and tender. Remove from the heat and stir in the Parmesan, the remaining 4 tablespoons butter, and the ground pepper. Serve at once.

# SPINACH AND FETA RICE

SERVES 6

2¼ cups chicken stock
½ cup basmati rice
½ cup white rice
1 tablespoon olive oil
1 medium onion, peeled and chopped
1 cup sliced mushrooms
2 cloves garlic, peeled and minced

6 cups chopped spinach, fresh or frozen
   and defrosted
2 teaspoons lemon juice
1 teaspoon dried oregano
6 ounces herbed feta cheese
Freshly ground black pepper, to taste

In a large saucepan over medium-high heat, bring the stock to a boil. Add both rices and stir until the stock resumes boiling. Reduce the heat, cover, and simmer for 45 minutes. Do not lift the lid; this is what makes rice gummy.

Meanwhile, in a large skillet over medium heat, warm the oil. Add the onion, mushrooms, garlic, and spinach. Stir in the lemon juice and oregano.

Fluff the cooked rice with a fork. Add it to the onion mixture along with the feta and ground pepper; toss gently.

# WILD RICE WITH DRIED CHERRIES

### SERVES 6 TO 8

Many thanks to Vince and Mary Pat Iaci of Seattle for this recipe. Just one of the many wonderful perks of my job!

6 tablespoons butter
4 green onions, thinly sliced
1 teaspoon dried thyme
½ pound wild rice blend *(see Note)*

6 cups chicken stock, heated
1 cup dried cherries
1 cup coarsely chopped roasted hazelnuts
¼ cup chopped parsley

In a large skillet over medium heat, melt the butter. Add the green onions and thyme; saute until the onions are limp. Add the wild rice blend and stir until the rice is coated. Slowly add the stock; increase the heat to high and bring to a boil, then reduce the heat to low and simmer, covered, for 45 minutes.

Remove from the heat and stir in the dried cherries, hazelnuts, and parsley. Serve hot.

*Note:* Wild rice blends are a mixture of long- and short-grained wild and white rices. You can find them in specialty stores and well-stocked supermarkets.

# COCONUT RICE

SERVES 6

Jasmine rice, from Thailand, is fragrant and full of flavor. It's a long-grained rice that graces any entree. I love to make it for curries, stir-fries, and, of course, Thai dishes.

1¾ cups water
¾ cup unsweetened coconut milk
⅛ teaspoon ground cardamom
1 teaspoon salt
1½ cups Jasmine rice

1 cup grated unsweetened coconut
½ red bell pepper, seeded and finely minced
½ yellow bell pepper, seeded and finely minced

In a large saucepan over high heat, combine the water, coconut milk, cardamom, and salt. Bring to a rolling boil. Add the rice and coconut; stir until the water returns to a boil, then cover, reduce the heat to low, and cook for 40 minutes.

Fluff the rice with a fork and gently fold in the bell peppers. Serve hot.

# Pasta

# POINTING THE WAY TO PERFECT PASTA

Pasta has become a staple in many kitchens in our hectic society. It's easy to prepare and it lends itself as readily to a simple, low-fat dinner as it does to a big, hearty meal or an elegant buffet. It can be prepared in a jiffy, and usually pleases even the most fussy eater. Here are some simple suggestions to help you make perfect pasta every time.

Use at least 4 cups water for every 4 ounces pasta. Keep the water at a rapid boil so that the pasta won't stick together and it can expand and cook evenly.

Add at least 1 tablespoon oil to the water to help prevent it from boiling over.

Add the pasta gradually, so that the water doesn't stop boiling. Cook uncovered, stirring occasionally.

When's the spaghetti ready? Remove one of the noodles from the water, cut it in half, and look for a solid white dot in the center. The minute the dot disappears, the pasta is done. Keep in mind that pasta continues to cook even after it's drained.

Drain the pasta but don't rinse it. Be sure to serve it on a heated plate.

If you're pressed for time, imitate the method used in restaurants. Partially cook the pasta ahead of time, then rinse in cold water to remove the starch. Toss in either butter, olive oil, or vegetable oil and set aside. Just before the pasta is to be served, pour it back into boiling water to complete the cooking. Drain, and serve with the desired sauce.

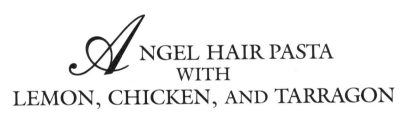

# ANGEL HAIR PASTA
## WITH
## LEMON, CHICKEN, AND TARRAGON

### SERVES 4

1 teaspoon salt
2 chicken breasts, boned, skinned, and cut
   into ½-inch chunks
2 tablespoons butter
½ cup chopped onion
Freshly grated zest of 1 large lemon
2½ tablespoons freshly squeezed lemon
   juice

2 tablespoons olive oil
1 tablespoon dried tarragon
2 teaspoons minced parsley
8 ounces angel hair pasta
Salt and freshly ground pepper, to taste
⅓ cup freshly grated Parmesan cheese

Salt the chicken breasts. In a large skillet over medium heat, melt the butter. Add the chicken and onion; saute until the onion is limp. Remove from the heat and add the lemon zest, lemon juice, olive oil, tarragon, and parsley. Stir to combine.

In a large pot of boiling salted water, cook the pasta until just tender. Drain in a colander, then transfer to the skillet with the chicken mixture. Toss well until the pasta is coated. Season with the salt and pepper and sprinkle with the Parmesan cheese.

# BAKED ZITI
## WITH
## ITALIAN SAUSAGE, ZUCCHINI, AND CREAM

SERVES 4

2 tablespoons olive oil
1 pound bulk Italian sausage
½ teaspoon dried red pepper flakes
½ cup chopped onion
2½ medium zucchini, trimmed and cut
    into ¼-inch slices
4 cloves garlic, peeled and minced
1 can (28 ounces) Italian plum tomatoes,
    drained and coarsely chopped

1½ cups whipping cream
1 teaspoon salt
2 teaspoons dried oregano
2 teaspoons dried basil
¼ teaspoon ground black pepper
12 ounces ziti pasta
3 tablespoons chopped fresh basil
Freshly grated Parmesan cheese, for
    sprinkling

In a large skillet over medium heat, warm the oil. Add the sausage and red pepper flakes; cook until the sausage is no longer pink. Add the onion, zucchini, and garlic; saute until the onion is limp and the sausage begins to brown. Add the tomatoes, cream, salt, oregano, dried basil, and ground pepper. Reduce the heat and simmer until the mixture thickens (about 5 minutes).

In a large pot of boiling salted water, cook the ziti until just tender. Drain. Add the pasta to the simmering sauce and toss until well combined and steaming. Garnish with the fresh basil and Parmesan cheese.

# CRAZY DAY CLAM SPAGHETTI

### SERVES 6

This is the perfect last-minute dinner. I make it whenever friends drop by unexpectedly, when nothing else sounds good, or when I'm on a tight schedule. I always have the ingredients on hand. In less than half an hour, I can make this dish, warm up a loaf of sourdough bread, and prepare a salad. If you have the time to make a dessert, try Cashmere Chocolate Truffle Cake.

½ cup plus 1 tablespoon olive oil
1 medium onion, peeled and finely
    chopped
3 cloves garlic, peeled and minced
5 ounces mushrooms, sliced
½ cup chopped fresh basil or 1 tablespoon
    dried basil
1 tablespoon dried oregano

Salt and pepper, to taste
½ cup dry white wine
2 cans (4½ ounces each) chopped clams,
    with liquid
1 tablespoon salt
1 pound spaghetti
1 cup chopped parsley
½ cup freshly grated Romano cheese

In a large skillet over medium heat, warm the ½ cup olive oil. Add the onion, garlic, and mushrooms; saute until the onions are limp. Add the basil, oregano, salt and pepper to taste, wine, and clams. Reduce the heat and simmer until some of the liquid evaporates.

Add the 1 tablespoon salt and the remaining 1 tablespoon oil to a large pot of boiling water. Add the spaghetti and cook until tender. Meanwhile, add the parsley and 3 tablespoons of the Romano cheese to the clam sauce; simmer for about 5 minutes.

Drain the pasta and stir it into the sauce. Sprinkle generously with the remaining cheese.

# FRESH TOMATO
## AND
## SMOKED MOZZARELLA PASTA

### SERVES 4 TO 6

This is a terrific dish for a hot summer evening. It also makes a delicious luncheon entree.

8 Italian plum tomatoes, seeded and chopped
½ cup olive oil
⅓ cup chopped fresh basil
1½ teaspoons dried oregano
Salt and freshly ground black pepper, to taste

½ cup freshly grated Parmesan cheese
¼ cup smoked mozzarella cheese cut into ¼-inch cubes
1 pound linguine

In a large glass serving bowl, combine the tomatoes, olive oil, basil, and oregano; toss gently. Sprinkle lightly with the salt and pepper. Add the Parmesan cheese, toss, and chill for at least 2 hours. Place the mozzarella in a large bowl; set aside.

Bring a large pot of salted water to boil; add the pasta slowly so that the water doesn't stop boiling; stir to prevent sticking. Cook until the pasta is just tender. Drain well and add to the mozzarella, tossing to melt the cheese slightly.

Add the pasta-mozzarella mixture to the marinated tomato mixture and toss until well combined. Serve immediately.

> *Cooking is like love. It should be entered into with abandon or not at all.*
> —Harriet Van Horne

# GNOCCHI WITH TOMATO CREAM SAUCE

SERVES 6

8 ounces mild goat cheese, such as
   Montrachet
1 egg plus 1 egg yolk
⅓ cup flour
1½ tablespoons freshly grated Romano
   cheese

TOMATO CREAM SAUCE

8 tablespoons butter
1½ cups heavy cream
½ teaspoon salt
½ teaspoon freshly ground black pepper

2 teaspoons salt
8 cups ice water
Fresh basil leaves, for garnish
Freshly grated Parmesan cheese, for
   sprinkling

¾ cup good-quality marinara sauce
2 tablespoons freshly grated Parmesan
   cheese

In a large bowl combine the goat cheese, egg, egg yolk, flour, and Romano cheese. Beat with a wooden spoon until the dough has the consistency of cream cheese (2 to 3 minutes). Chill until firm.

In a large skillet bring 2 inches of water to a boil with the salt. Reduce the heat until the salted water is simmering. Put the ice water in a large bowl.

Fill a teaspoon with the chilled dough, then divide the dough in half and slide each half off the spoon and into the simmering water. Cook until the gnocchi floats, then with a slotted spoon transfer the gnocchi to the ice water. Repeat until all the dough is used. Drain in a colander.

Prepare the Tomato Cream Sauce and keep warm. Transfer the gnocchi to a steamer basket over simmering water and steam until they are warm (4 to 5 minutes). Spoon the warm sauce into 6 soup bowls. Place 5 or 6 gnocchi on top of the sauce in each bowl. Garnish with the basil and sprinkle with the freshly grated Parmesan.

*Tomato Cream Sauce:* In a large skillet over medium heat, melt the butter. Add the cream; bring to a boil, then reduce the heat and simmer until the mixture is reduced to ⅔ cup (about 10 minutes). Season with the salt and pepper. Whisk in the marinara sauce and Parmesan cheese.

# LINGUINE WITH GORGONZOLA CREAM SAUCE

SERVES 4

This dish is very rich, so serve light accompaniments with it. A simple tossed salad with raspberry vinaigrette and a loaf of crusty French bread is all you need. Try Fresh Pineapple and Dried Cherries in Port for a simple yet elegant dessert.

1¼ cups whipping cream
8 ounces Gorgonzola cheese, cut into
   pieces
1¼ pounds linguine
Freshly ground black pepper, to taste

⅓ cup chopped pecans
⅓ cup pine nuts
⅓ cup chopped hazelnuts
¾ cup freshly grated Parmesan cheese

In a large skillet over medium heat, warm the cream. Gradually add the Gorgonzola cheese; stir until the mixture is well blended and creamy (about 3 minutes).

Cook the linguine in a large pot of boiling salted water until just tender. Drain. Add the pasta to the cheese sauce and toss until well coated. Season with the ground pepper. Just before serving, sprinkle the pasta with the nuts and Parmesan cheese.

# MUSHROOM-ONION CARBONARA

### SERVES 4

In the mid 1970s I worked for *Sunset* magazine. They used employees as models, and I was chosen to help cook and eat this pasta dish for the photographs in an article on pasta. Every now and then I come across an old copy of the magazine when I'm looking through boxes in the barn; there I am, holding a fork full of pasta to my grinning mouth. It makes me feel very silly—until I remember how much I've enjoyed making this recipe. I think about how much I've changed in twenty years, and I'm thankful that this pasta dish has only improved with the passing of time.

8 tablespoons butter
2 large onions, peeled and thinly sliced
1 pound mushrooms, sliced
2 cloves garlic, peeled and minced
¾ cup chopped parsley, plus more for garnish
4 eggs, well beaten

2 cups freshly grated Parmesan cheese, plus more for garnish
6 ounces regular fettuccine
6 ounces whole wheat, tomato, or spinach fettuccine
Salt and freshly ground black pepper, to taste

In a large skillet over medium heat, melt 4 tablespoons of the butter. Add the onions; cover and cook until limp, stirring often. Uncover and cook until golden. Add the mushrooms and garlic. Saute until almost all the mushroom liquid has evaporated; set aside and keep warm. Place the ¾ cup parsley, the eggs, and the 2 cups Parmesan in separate bowls; set aside.

Cook both pastas in a large pot of boiling salted water until just tender. Drain, then return to the pot and add the remaining 4 tablespoons butter. Toss until well combined. Add half of the parsley, eggs, and Parmesan; with pasta forks or big wooden spoons, lift and toss until well combined. Add the remaining parsley, eggs, and cheese and toss again. Add the reserved mushroom mixture; contintue lifting and tossing. Garnish with the chopped parsley and Parmesan, then sprinkle with the salt and pepper. Serve hot.

# HEARTY RED WINE FETTUCCINE

### SERVES 4

½ pound thickly sliced bacon
3 tablespoons olive oil
1 large onion, peeled and chopped
1 cup mushrooms, sliced
4 cloves garlic, peeled and minced
5 large tomatoes, peeled, seeded, and
    chopped
½ cup dry, hearty red wine, or to taste
2 teaspoons salt

1 tablespoon dried tarragon
¼ teaspoon red pepper flakes
1 teaspoon freshly ground black pepper
1 teaspoon sugar
⅓ cup chopped parsley
12 ounces fettuccine
2 tablespoons butter
½ cup freshly grated Parmesan cheese

In a large skillet over medium hat, fry the bacon until crisp. Drain on paper towels, crumble, and set aside.

Pour out all but 1 tablespoon of the bacon drippings. Add the olive oil, onion, and mushrooms. Saute about 5 minutes.

Add the garlic, tomatoes, and wine. Reduce the heat and simmer, then add the salt, tarragon, red pepper flakes, ground pepper, and sugar. Cover and simmer for 25 minutes, stirring occasionally. Add the parsley and crumbled bacon; keep warm.

Cook the fettuccine in a large pot of boiling salted water until just tender. Drain, then return the pasta to the pot and toss with the butter. Add the wine sauce and toss to coat the pasta. Top with the grated Parmesan.

# Desserts

# AMARETTO CHOCOLATE SILK

SERVES 6

1 packet unflavored gelatin
2 tablespoons water
1½ cups whipping cream
½ cup granulated sugar
4 ounces semisweet chocolate chips

4 ounces milk chocolate chips
4 tablespoons Amaretto liqueur
1¼ cups sour cream
Shaved chocolate, for garnish

TOPPING

½ cup whipping cream
2 tablespoons Amaretto liqueur

2 tablespoons confectioners' sugar

In a large saucepan combine the gelatin and the water; let stand for 5 minutes. Add the whipping cream, granulated sugar, and chocolate chips; cook over medium heat, stirring frequently, until the chocolate is completely melted (4 to 6 minutes). Remove from the heat and let cool until lukewarm. Stir in the Amaretto and sour cream. Pour into wine or parfait glasses. Cover and chill until firm.

Prepare the Topping. Spoon it onto each dessert and garnish with the shaved chocolate.

*Topping:* Whip the cream until thickened but not forming peaks. Gently fold in the Amaretto and confectioners' sugar.

# ANGELA PIA

SERVES 8

In Italian, Angela Pia translates to "angel's pie"; it certainly tastes like a slice of heaven. This was my favorite dessert as a child, and it still tops my list. The flavor is delicate and the texture is light and creamy. Angela Pia is a wonderful finish to any meal.

1 tablespoon unflavored gelatin
¼ cup cold water
3 eggs, separated
½ cup superfine sugar

1 cup heavy cream
¼ cup brandy
¼ cup rum
1 tablespoon vanilla extract

In a large saucepan combine the gelatin and the water. Stir until the gelatin has dissolved, then place over medium heat and cook until the gelatin has melted. Set aside until cool (about 5 minutes).

Beat the egg whites until very stiff peaks form; set aside.

In a large bowl whisk the yolks, gradually adding the sugar until the yolks are thick and creamy yellow. Stir in the melted gelatin.

In another large bowl whip the cream until stiff; slowly add the brandy, rum, and vanilla.

Gently fold the beaten egg whites and the whipped cream mixture into the gelatin mixture. Pour into parfait or wine glasses. Chill before serving.

# CAFE AU LAIT POTS-DE-CREME

SERVES 6

2¼ cups milk
1¼ tablespoons freeze-dried coffee crystals
7 egg yolks, at room temperature
½ cup plus 2 tablespoons sugar

Whipped cream, for garnish
Chocolate-covered espresso beans or
  chocolate coffee beans, for garnish

Preheat the oven to 325°F. In a large saucepan over medium heat, bring the milk just to a boil. Whisk in the coffee crystals and remove from the heat.

In a large bowl gently whisk the yolks. Add the sugar and whisk until blended. Add 1 cup of the milk mixture, whisking gently. With a wooden spoon gradually stir in the remaining milk mixture.

Strain the custard mixture into a large measuring cup or bowl with a spout. Let stand about 5 minutes, then skim the foamy bubbles off the surface.

Place 6 small ramekins in a roasting pan. Pour the custard mixture into the ramekins; skim the foam off the surface again if needed. Place in the oven and add boiling water to the roasting pan to come halfway up the sides of the ramekins. Place a piece of aluminum foil on top of the ramekins. Bake until the tops of the custards are set and the point of a small knife inserted in the center comes out clean (about 40 minutes). Remove the ramekins from the roasting pan and let cool, then cover and refrigerate for at least 3 hours.

Let the custards stand for 15 minutes at room temperature before serving. Garnish with the whipped cream and chocolate-covered beans.

> *I think if I were a woman I'd wear coffee as a perfume.*
> —John Van Druten (1901–1957)

# RANGE MARMALADE SOUFFLE

### SERVES 4

The most memorable character, and well as the best cook, I've ever had the pleasure of meeting is Dagny Sundin. At eighty-four, Dagny still has a spring in her step and a mischievous sparkle in her eyes. I wish I had met Dagny twenty-five years ago; she is a woman who knows food inside and out. She started cooking and catering in the 1920s and has created some fabulous meals. Dagny made this dessert for us one evening, and I've been making it ever since. Each time I serve this, I think of Dagny and feel blessed to know her.

Butter, for double boiler
4 egg whites, at room temperature
4 tablespoons granulated sugar
4 tablespoons good-quality orange
  marmalade

2 cups whipping cream
4 egg yolks
3 tablespoons confectioners' sugar
¼ cup Grand Marnier or Cointreau

Generously butter the top of a double boiler; set aside. In a large bowl whip the egg whites until stiff peaks form. Gradually add the granulated sugar and marmalade; whip until the meringue mixture is dry and very stiff.

Pour the meringue mixture into the top of the prepared double boiler and place over boiling water. Reduce the heat and simmer for 1½ hours. DON'T LIFT THE LID AT ANY TIME! The lid will start to lift off as the souffle expands, but that's all right.

In the meantime, in a large bowl whip the cream to soft peaks. Add the yolks, one at a time. Stir in the confectioners' sugar and Grand Marnier, then whip again until soft peaks form.

Remove the pan with the meringue mixture from the top of the double boiler; quickly turn the mixture into a large bowl. Then spoon the meringue into individual bowls and serve warm with the Grand Marnier sauce.

# FRESH LEMON MOUSSE
## WITH
## MARIONBERRY SAUCE

SERVES 8

I love anything lemon. I would bathe in it if I could. But our friend Stewart's passion for lemon surpasses even mine. So Stewart, this one's for you. Pucker up—it's as lemony as it gets.

6 large eggs
4 egg yolks
1½ cups sugar
1¼ cups freshly squeezed lemon juice
1½ tablespoons freshly grated lemon zest
14 tablespoons unsalted butter, chilled and
   cut into small pieces

¾ cup whipping cream
1½ cups fresh marionberries
3 tablespoons sugar, or more to taste
Mint sprigs or lemon slices, for garnish

In a heavy saucepan whisk the eggs and yolks until foamy. Blend in the 1½ cups sugar, lemon juice, and zest. Cook over low heat, stirring constantly, until the mixture thickens to the consistency of a heavy custard. Do not allow to boil.

Remove the mixture from the heat and whisk in the butter. Transfer to a large bowl and let cool until thick, stirring occasionally.

Whip the cream until soft peaks form, then fold very gently into the lemon mixture until just combined. Spoon the mousse into parfait or wine glasses, then cover and chill until set.

In a medium bowl mash the marionberries with a fork. Mix in the 3 tablespoons sugar. You may wish to add more sugar if the berries are very tart. Chill. Spoon the berry sauce over the lemon mousse; garnish with a mint sprig.

# CHOCOLATE PECAN PIE

SERVES 8 TO 10

Remember, when you're cooking with chocolate, always wear brown!

4 large eggs
2 egg yolks
1½ cups light corn syrup
1 cup granulated sugar
1 cup packed brown sugar

3 tablespoons butter, melted
1 tablespoon molasses
1¼ teaspoons vanilla extract
6 ounces semisweet chocolate, chopped
1¼ cups chopped pecans

CRUST

1½ cups flour
⅛ teaspoon salt
1 teaspoon instant espresso powder

3 tablespoons butter, cut into small pieces
2 tablespoons vegetable shortening, chilled
Water, as needed

Preheat the oven to 350°F. Prepare the Crust. Roll out the chilled dough on a well-floured work surface. Transfer to a 9-inch pie plate with 2-inch-high sides. Crimp the edges decoratively.

In a large bowl whisk the eggs and yolks until frothy. Add the corn syrup, granulated sugar, brown sugar, butter, molasses, and vanilla; blend well.

Place the chocolate and pecans in the prepared pie crust, then pour in the egg mixture. Bake on the middle rack of the oven until the top of the pie is dry and firm to the touch (about 1 hour and 10 minutes). Let cool completely before cutting.

*Crust:* In the work bowl of a food processor, combine the flour, salt, and espresso powder. Add the butter and shortening a little at a time; process until crumbly. Add enough water to form a dough that holds together. Shape it into a ball, enclose in plastic wrap, and chill.

# FRESH PEACH PIE EXTRAORDINAIRE

SERVES 6 TO 8

**8 medium ripe peaches, peeled and sliced**

CRUST

**2 cups flour, whisked until light**
**3 tablespoons confectioners' sugar**
**1 teaspoon salt**
**8 tablespoons butter, chilled**
**¼ cup solid vegetable shortening, chilled**

**2 teaspoons freshly grated lemon zest**
**¼ cup peach nectar, well chilled**
**1½ tablespoons freshly squeezed lemon juice, or as needed**

GLAZE

**1½ cups peach nectar**
**¾ cup peach jam**

**2¼ tablespoons rum**

Preheat the oven to 425°F. Prepare the Crust. Roll out the dough on a lightly floured work surface to ¼ inch thick. Press the dough gently into a 9-inch deep-dish pie pan or a tart pan with a removable bottom. Trim the edges of the dough and crimp decoratively. Freeze for 1 hour, then bake on the middle rack of the oven until golden (18 to 20 minutes).

Prepare the Glaze. Brush the bottom and sides of the Crust with the Glaze. Starting in the middle of the crust, begin placing the peach slices in a circular pattern until all the slices are used. (Make a double layer with any extra slices.) Brush with the remaining Glaze, making sure that all the peaches are covered. Chill before serving.

*Crust:* In a large bowl combine the flour, confectioners' sugar, and salt. With a pastry blender cut in the butter and shortening. Add the lemon zest and toss lightly. Gradually add the peach nectar, blending gently but thoroughly. Add enough lemon juice to make a firm dough. Form into a ball, enclose with plastic wrap, and chill.

*Glaze:* In a small saucepan over medium heat, combine all the ingredients; stir to blend, then cook until reduced to about ¾ cup (35 to 40 minutes). Strain and keep warm.

# MY FAVORITE APPLE PIE

SERVES 8

8 McIntosh or Granny Smith apples,
    peeled, cored, and sliced
2 cups sour cream
1 cup granulated sugar

⅓ cup flour
1 egg
2½ teaspoons vanilla extract
½ teaspoon salt

CRUST

2 cups flour
⅓ cup granulated sugar
1¼ teaspoons ground cinnamon

½ teaspoon salt
10 tablespoons butter
⅓ cup apple cider or apple juice

TOPPING

½ cup flour
⅓ cup packed brown sugar
⅓ cup granulated sugar

1 tablespoon ground cinnamon
⅛ teaspoon salt
8 tablespoons butter, at room temperature

Preheat the oven to 450°F. In a large bowl combine all the filling ingredients and mix well. Prepare the Crust and spoon the filling into it. Bake for 10 minutes, then reduce the heat to 350°F and continue baking until the filling is slightly puffed and golden brown (about 40 minutes longer).

Meanwhile, prepare the Topping. Spoon it over the pie and bake 12 to 15 minutes longer.

*Crust:* In the work bowl of a food processor, combine the flour, granulated sugar,

cinnamon, and salt. Blend in the butter a bit at a time. Add the cider and whirl until the dough holds together. Remove from the work bowl and form into a ball. Transfer to a floured work surface and roll out in a circle that is slightly larger than a 10-inch deep-dish pie plate. Gently transfer the dough to the pie plate and crimp the edges decoratively.

*Topping:* In a small bowl combine the flour, sugars, cinnamon, and salt. Blend in the butter until the mixture is crumbly.

# FROZEN KIWI, LIME, AND RASPBERRY TART

SERVES 6 TO 8

This refreshing, low-fat dessert works as well on a hot summer evening as it does in a holiday dessert buffet. The colors make it very festive.

**Lime slices, fresh raspberries, and kiwifruit slices, for garnish**

CRUST

**1 cup graham cracker crumbs**

**2 tablespoons butter, melted**

KIWI MIXTURE

**5 kiwifruits, peeled**
**1½ cups water**
**½ cup sugar**

**3 tablespoons corn syrup**
**Juice of 2 limes**
**1 tablespoon freshly grated lime zest**

RASPBERRY MIXTURE

**¾ cup raspberry puree**
**1 cup water**
**⅓ cup sugar**

**2 tablespoons corn syrup**
**Juice of 1 lime**
**½ tablespoon freshly grated lime zest**

Prepare the Crust, Kiwi Mixture, and Raspberry Mixture. Spoon the Kiwi Mixture into the frozen crust, patting it up along the sides and leaving a hole in the middle for the Raspberry Mixture. Spoon the Raspberry Mixture into the center of the Kiwi Mixture. Freeze the tart for at least 2 hours. Garnish with the lime slices, fresh raspberries, and kiwifruit slices.

*Crust:* Combine the graham cracker crumbs and butter; press into just the bottom of a

deep tart pan or a 9-inch pie plate. Freeze until firm.

*Kiwi Mixture:* In the work bowl of a food processor, combine all the ingredients. Process until the sugar is dissolved. Pour into a shallow pan and freeze until firm but not solid (1 to 2 hours). With an electric mixer beat until light but still frozen.

*Raspberry Mixture:* Prepare the same way as for the Kiwi Mixture.

# LEMON TART

SERVES 6 TO 8

This is the dessert I make most frequently. It's my "good old standby" and hasn't failed me yet. I've never served it to anyone who didn't like it, and it fits my criteria for a truly great dessert: it's simple to make, it doesn't take long to put together, and—best of all—it's lemon. *Bon Appetit* magazine has requested this recipe, and I'm eagerly waiting for it to be printed. I'm sure that when it is, between my mother and me, we'll buy most of the available copies in Washington state!

8 ounces cream cheese
¾ cup granulated sugar
3 eggs
1½ tablespoons freshly grated lemon zest

⅔ cup freshly squeezed lemon juice
Sweetened whipping cream, for garnish
Sliced lemon, for garnish

CRUST

¾ cup flour
6 tablespoons butter, chilled

3½ tablespoons confectioners' sugar

Preheat the oven to 350°F. Prepare the Crust. In a large bowl beat the cream cheese until smooth. Blend in the granulated sugar, eggs, zest, and lemon juice. Pour into the prebaked Crust and bake until the filling is set (about 25 minutes). Let cool at room temperature, then chill until serving time. Garnish with the sweetened whipping cream and lemon slices.

*Crust:* In a medium bowl or the work bowl of a food processor, combine all the ingredients and mix until the dough forms a loose ball. Press the dough firmly into a 9-inch tart pan. Freeze for 1 hour, then bake at 425°F until lightly browned (about 8 minutes). Let cool.

# CASHMERE CHOCOLATE TRUFFLE CAKE

SERVES 6 TO 8

Instead of serving this with whipped cream, as called for here, you could use fresh berries or a berry puree. Simply drizzle the puree on the plate before serving, then place a slice of the torte on top. Garnish with a fresh berry.

8 tablespoons unsalted butter, plus butter for pan
16 ounces semisweet chocolate
1½ teaspoons flour
1½ teaspoons sugar

1 teaspoon hot water
4 eggs, separated
1 cup whipping cream, sweetened and whipped, for accompaniment

Preheat the oven to 425°F. Butter the bottom of an 8-inch springform pan; set aside. In the top of a double boiler over simmering water, melt the chocolate and the 8 tablespoons butter. Add the flour, sugar, and hot water; blend well. Remove from the heat and set aside.

In a small bowl combine the egg yolks with a small amount of the chocolate mixture; blend well. (This will warm the yolks sufficiently so that they won't cook when added to the hot chocolate mixture.) Gradually add the yolk mixture to the chocolate mixture, beating well after each addition.

Beat the egg whites until stiff. Fold gently into the yolk-chocolate mixture, then turn into the prepared pan. Bake for 15 minutes. The cake will look uncooked in the center, but trust me on this. Remove from the oven and let cool completely, then chill. Cut into slices and serve with the whipped cream.

# FAYE'S RED VELVET CAKE

SERVES 8

This is without a doubt my favorite cake. The frosting tastes like whipped cream, and the cake is moist, with an underlying chocolate flavor. Its attractive red color makes it perfect for Valentine's Day.

1½ cups sugar
½ cup solid vegetable shortening
2 eggs
2 tablespoons cocoa
2 ounces red food coloring
1 teaspoon salt

1 teaspoon vanilla extract
1 cup buttermilk
2½ cups cake flour
1½ tablespoons distilled white vinegar
1 teaspoon baking soda

FROSTING

5 tablespoons flour
1 cup milk
1 cup butter

1 cup sugar
1½ teaspoons vanilla extract

In a large bowl cream together the sugar and shortening. Add the eggs and beat well. Make a paste of the cocoa and food coloring; add to the creamed mixture.

Stir the salt and vanilla into the buttermilk. Add to the creamed mixture alternately with the sifted cake flour. Combine the vinegar and baking soda; gently fold into the batter. Don't overblend; it will make the batter tough.

Preheat the oven to 350°F. Generously grease and flour two 9-inch cake pans. Pour in the batter and bake until the cake pulls away from the edges of the pan or the top springs back when lightly touched (25 to 30 minutes).

To assemble, cut enough off the tops of the cakes to make them even. Place the surplus cake in the work bowl of a food processor and blend until fine crumbs form; set aside. Prepare the Frosting. Frost the sides and top of each cake. Very gently press the reserved cake crumbs into the sides of the cake until the sides are completely covered with crumbs. Chill.

*Frosting:* In a small saucepan over medium heat, whisk together the flour and milk; cook until thickened. Chill. In a small bowl cream together the butter, sugar, and vanilla. Add to the flour mixture and beat with a mixer to the consistency of whipped cream.

# CRAN-RASPBERRY LINZER TORTE

SERVES 6 TO 8

½ cup water
3 cups fresh or frozen cranberries
1 cup granulated sugar
1 tablespoon freshly grated orange zest

⅔ cup raspberry preserves
Confectioners' sugar, for dusting top of
    torte

CRUST

2½ cups butter, at room temperature
1 cup granulated sugar
2 teaspoons freshly grated orange zest
2 eggs

1¼ cups finely ground almonds
2 teaspoons ground cinnamon
½ teaspoon ground cloves
¼ teaspoon salt

In a 2- to 2½-quart saucepan over high heat, bring the water to a boil. Add the cranberries, granulated sugar, and zest. Boil, uncovered, until the mixture has the consistency of soft jam (about 10 minutes). Stir in the preserves; let cool.

Preheat the oven to 325°F. Prepare the Crust. Press three-fourths of the dough into a 9-inch tart pan with a removable bottom. Spread the cran-raspberry mixture over the bottom of the crust. Transfer the remaining dough to a pastry bag and squirt a circle of dough around the edge, then squeeze out a lattice pattern on top. (Try to keep the strips thin; the dough will spread as it bakes.) Bake on the middle rack of the oven until the lattice is nicely browned and the filling is bubbly (about 50 minutes). Remove from the oven and let cool, then sprinkle with the confectioners' sugar.

*Crust:* In the work bowl of a food processor, cream together the butter and granulated sugar until light. Add the zest and eggs; process until well combined. Add the ground almonds, cinnamon, cloves, and salt; whirl until well blended.

# FESTIVE PUMPKIN CHEESECAKE

### SERVES 12

16 ounces cream cheese, at room
   temperature
1 cup half-and-half
1 cup canned pumpkin
1 cup sugar
4 eggs, separated
3 tablespoons flour

1½ teaspoons vanilla extract
1 teaspoon ground cinnamon
½ teaspoon ground ginger
½ teaspoon ground nutmeg
¼ teaspoon salt
Freshly grated nutmeg, for garnish

CRUST

½ cups crushed gingersnaps
3½ tablespoons butter, melted

½ teaspoon ground cinnamon

TOPPING

1 cup sour cream
2 tablespoons sugar

1 teaspoon vanilla extract

Prepare the Crust; set aside.

In the work bowl of a food processor, whip
the cream cheese. Slowly add the half-and-
half. Add the pumpkin, sugar, egg yolks,
flour, vanilla, cinnamon, ginger, nutmeg, and
salt; process until smooth. Transfer to a large
bowl.

Beat the egg whites until stiff. Fold them into
the pumpkin mixture, then turn into the
prebaked Crust and bake for 1 hour longer.

Meanwhile, prepare the Topping. Spread it
over the baked cheesecake and return to the
oven for 5 minutes longer.

Remove the cheesecake from the oven and let
it cool for 30 minutes. Unhinge the sides of
the springform pan from the bottom and let
the cheesecake stand for another 30 minutes
before completely removing the sides of the
pan. Let cool for 2 hours longer, then cover
and refrigerate. Garnish with the freshly
grated nutmeg.

*Crust:* Preheat the oven to 325°F. Combine
the gingersnaps, butter, and cinnamon. Press
into the bottom and 2 inches up the sides of
a 9-inch springform pan. Bake for 5 minutes.

*Topping:* Combine all the ingredients and mix
well.

# CHOCOLATE SURPRISE CUPCAKES

## MAKES 2 DOZEN

These cupcakes are wonderful for picnics, barbecues, potlucks, or just having around the house. The first time I served them was at my husband's thirty-fifth birthday party. One of the guests came into the kitchen saying, "I don't even like cupcakes, and I've already eaten six! Please give my wife this recipe." His wife found me later and told me that he wouldn't let her leave without it. I don't think I could find a better recommendation.

3 cups flour
2 cups sugar
2 cups water
½ cup cocoa
⅔ cup oil

2 teaspoons baking soda
2 tablespoons distilled white vinegar
2 teaspoons vanilla extract
1 teaspoon salt

FILLING

8 ounces cream cheese
1 egg

⅓ cup sugar
1 cup chocolate chips, coarsely chopped

Preheat the oven to 325°F. Prepare the Filling and set aside.

In a large bowl combine all the ingredients. Line muffin tins with paper liners. Fill each muffin cup half full with batter, then take

1 heaping teaspoon Filling and gently push it into the middle of each cupcake. Top with the remaining batter. Bake until a toothpick inserted comes out clean (about 25 minutes).

*Filling:* Cream together all the ingredients.

# STRAWBERRY-RHUBARB COBBLER WITH COOKIE DOUGH CRUST

SERVES 6

I never seem to have enough rhubarb, which grows wild in our garden. It has a tart, refreshing flavor, different from any other fruit. I use it in muffins and in sauces, but I think pairing it with strawberries makes an unbeatable combination. The crisp and buttery shortbread crust of this cobbler is reminiscent of sugar cookies. You can make this in the early summer when strawberries and rhubarb are at their best; freeze it before baking it. Whenever you want some in fall or winter, take it out of the freezer and bake as directed. It's a pleasant reminder and a wonderful taste of sunshine.

2 pints fresh strawberries, hulled and
    thickly sliced
6 cups fresh rhubarb cut into ½-inch-thick
    slices

1½ cups sugar
3 tablespoons quick-cooking tapioca

TOPPING

1 cup flour
½ teaspoon baking powder
⅛ teaspoon salt
1 cup butter, softened

1⅓ cups sugar
1 egg
1 teaspoon almond extract

Preheat the oven to 400°F. Generously grease a 13- by 9-inch baking dish; set aside.

In a large bowl combine the strawberries, rhubarb, sugar, and tapioca; let stand for 15 minutes. Transfer to the greased baking dish.

Prepare the Topping. Drop by tablespoonfuls on the strawberry-rhubarb mixture. Bake

until the top is golden and the sides are bubbly (35 to 45 minutes).

*Topping:* In a small bowl combine the flour, baking powder, and salt; whisk until light. In another small bowl cream together the butter and sugar, then blend in the egg and almond extract.

# ED WINE SHERBET

### SERVES 4

This is the most simple dessert imaginable. It's refreshing after a heavy dinner, or a pleasant way to end a light lunch. It's also fat-free, so make a double batch!

**1 pint raspberry sherbet**
**2 teaspoons freshly grated orange zest**

**2 tablespoons freshly squeezed orange juice**
**½ cup Sangria**

In a large bowl combine the sherbet, zest, and juice; beat until creamy. Gradually add the Sangria. Pour into wine glasses and freeze.

# Fruit

# FRESH FRUIT WITH CREME FRAICHE AND AMARETTO

SERVES 4 TO 6

Creme fraiche is a tremendously versatile item to have in your refrigerator. You can use it in sauces, dollop it over fresh fruit, fish, or vegetables, and use it as a base for salad dressings. It is available commercially, or you can use this recipe to make your own.

3 or 4 ripe peaches, peeled and sliced
1 pint raspberries
1 pint blueberries

¼ cup sugar
⅓ cup Amaretto liqueur

CREME FRAICHE

¼ cup buttermilk

1 cup heavy cream

Prepare the Creme Fraiche and set aside. In a large bowl combine the peaches, berries, sugar, and liqueur. Stir gently so you don't bruise the berries. Chill. Serve in wine glasses with a dollop of the Creme Fraiche.

*Creme Fraiche:* In a medium bowl combine the buttermilk and cream. Cover and let stand at room temperature for 12 hours, then chill. This will keep about 1 week in the refrigerator.

# FRESH PINEAPPLE AND DRIED CHERRIES IN PORT

SERVES 4 TO 6

This not only makes a refreshing dessert, it is also wonderful as a first course for breakfast or brunch.

2½ cups tawny port
½ cup sugar
¼ teaspoon whole peppercorns
8 whole cloves

1 stick cinnamon
½ cup dried cherries
1 whole pineapple, peeled, cored, and cut into 1-inch chunks

In a large saucepan over medium heat, combine the port, sugar, peppercorns, cloves, and cinnamon. Bring to a boil, then reduce the heat and simmer for 10 minutes.

Remove from the heat and stir in the cherries and pineapple. Chill for at least 12 hours.

# STRAWBERRY PARFAITS

SERVES 4 TO 6

This is the most common first course we serve at Cashmere Country Inn. Fresh peaches, apricots, cantaloupe, or bananas are fine alternatives to berries.

**2 pints fresh strawberries, sliced, or
  1 package (10 ounces) frozen sliced
  strawberries, defrosted
½ cup sugar**

**1 cup granola
1 cup vanilla yogurt, or more as needed
4 to 6 strawberries, sliced, for garnish**

Place the 2 pints strawberries in a large bowl and gently stir in the sugar; set aside.

Place about 1 tablespoon granola in each parfait or wine glass. To each add 1 tablespoon vanilla yogurt, or more to taste. Top with some of the sweetened berries. Repeat, finishing with a sliced berry layer. Top with a dollop of yogurt and garnish with a sliced strawberry.

# *Muffins, Breads, Pastries, and Spreads*

❖

# MUCH ADO ABOUT MUFFINS

Around the Cashmere Country Inn, muffins are the bread of life. One day I sat down and tried to figure out just how many muffins I've made over the last five and a half years. I gave up. Needless to say, it was several thousand! While I don't consider myself an expert, I do feel that I have enough experience in this one area to pass along some tips to help you create wonderful muffins.

1.  Always preheat the oven, so once you've filled the muffin cups you can pop them directly into the oven without delay.

2.  This is the most important tip I can impart to you: don't overmix the batter. Most of the time you'll be combining the dry ingredients and wet ingredients separately, then blending them together. When you do incorporate the two, stir gently, quickly, and for no more than 15 to 20 seconds. If you have additions to the batter such as nuts or fruit, fold them in gently.

3.  For an average-sized muffin with a lovely raised crown, fill each cup about three-fourths full. If you like a crusty muffin top and a more cakelike bottom, fill the cups higher and sprinkle with granulated sugar.

4.  Sometimes you'll have a little more or less batter than what the recipe estimates. If you have extra and don't want to bother with another muffin pan, or don't have one, simply bake the batter in a greased custard cup. If you do use an extra muffin pan, be sure to fill the empty muffin cups with a few tablespoons of water to ensure even baking.

5.  To test for doneness, I simply touch the tops of the muffins. Another way is to smell them. When the aroma starts filling the kitchen, check the muffins because they'll be done, or very close to it. A more scientific method is to insert a sharp knife or wooden pick into one of the muffins. If it comes out clean, the muffins are done.

6.  Always let the muffins rest a few minutes before serving. If you take them out of the pan too soon, sometimes the muffins will still be too hot to have set (especially those containing fruit) and will fall apart. And if you pull the muffin paper off while the muffin is too warm, half of the muffin will stick to the paper.

7.  Muffins are usually best served slightly warm.

# FRESH APPLE MUFFINS

MAKES 18 MUFFINS

1½ cups packed brown sugar
⅔ cup vegetable oil
1 egg
1 cup buttermilk
1½ teaspoons vanilla extract
1 teaspoon baking soda

1 teaspoon salt
½ teaspoon ground cinnamon
2½ cups flour
1½ cups diced apple
½ cup chopped walnuts

TOPPING

⅓ cup granulated sugar
1 teaspoon butter, melted

½ teaspoon ground cinnamon

Preheat the oven to 375°F. Prepare the Topping and set aside.

In a large bowl combine the brown sugar, oil, egg, buttermilk, and vanilla. In a medium bowl combine the baking soda, salt, cinnamon, and flour; add to the egg mixture. Gently fold in the apple and nuts. Divide the batter evenly among prepared muffin cups and sprinkle with the Topping. Bake until a toothpick inserted comes out clean (18 to 20 minutes).

*Topping:* Combine the granulated sugar, butter, and cinnamon; mix well.

# COCONUT MUFFINS

MAKES 15 TO 18 MUFFINS

These muffins taste like a cross between coconut cream pie and coconut cake. Delicious!

1 cup milk
2 eggs
½ cup vegetable oil
1½ teaspoons vanilla extract
3 cups flour
2 cups unsweetened shredded coconut

1¼ cups packed brown sugar
1 teaspoon baking powder
1 teaspoon baking soda
1 teaspoon salt
1½ teaspoons freshly grated nutmeg

TOPPING

1 tablespoon granulated sugar
1 teaspoon freshly grated nutmeg

⅛ cup coconut

Preheat the oven to 400°F. Prepare the Topping and set aside.

In a small bowl combine the milk, eggs, oil, and vanilla. In a large bowl combine the flour, coconut, brown sugar, baking powder, baking soda, salt, and nutmeg; whisk together until thoroughly blended and the coconut doesn't clump. (I usually use my fingers to remove the lumps.)

Create a well in the center of the flour mixture and pour in the egg mixture. Gently fold in the egg mixture. Divide the batter evenly among prepared muffin cups. Sprinkle with the Topping and bake until lightly golden (18 to 20 minutes).

*Topping:* Combine the granulated sugar, nutmeg, and coconut; mix well.

# HOLIDAY EGGNOG MUFFINS

### MAKES 12 MUFFINS

2 cups flour
¾ cup granulated sugar
1¾ teaspoons baking powder
½ teaspoon salt
1½ cups eggnog

8 tablespoons butter, melted
2 eggs
1 teaspoon vanilla extract
½ teaspoon freshly grated nutmeg

TOPPING

1 cup flour
⅓ cup butter, softened

⅓ cup packed brown sugar
½ teaspoon freshly grated nutmeg

Preheat the oven to 400°F. Prepare the Topping and set aside.

In a large bowl combine the flour, granulated sugar, baking powder, and salt; whisk together until light. In a small bowl combine the eggnog, butter, eggs, vanilla, and nutmeg; add to the flour mixture. Divide the batter evenly among prepared muffin cups and sprinkle with the Topping. Bake until a toothpick inserted comes out clean (18 to 20 minutes).

*Topping:* Combine the flour, butter, brown sugar, and nutmeg; mix well.

# FRESH CHERRY MUFFINS

MAKES 24 MUFFINS

Every year in June, I and our dedicated employee Julie do what we refer to as "cherry patrol." Not our favorite chore, it's washing, pitting, and slicing the cherries we freeze for these muffins. This year we did 100 pounds. After hours of this, we looked frightful—spattered with cherry juice from head to toe. My hands are usually cherry stained for weeks afterward. I eat the big juicy cherries as I go, and by the time "cherry patrol" is over, I'm so full (and tired) of cherries, it carries me over to the next year!

8 tablespoons butter, melted
2 eggs
1½ cups sugar, plus more for sprinkling
1 cup milk
2 teaspoons almond extract

3 cups flour
2½ teaspoons baking powder
¾ teaspoon salt
⅛ teaspoon baking soda
2 cups pitted fresh cherries

Preheat the oven to 400°F. In a medium bowl cream together the butter, eggs, and the 1½ cups sugar. Add the milk and almond extract. In a large bowl combine the flour, baking powder, salt, and baking soda.

Make a well in the flour mixture and add the egg mixture. Stir just until combined, then gently fold in the cherries. Divide evenly among prepared muffin cups, sprinkle with the sugar, and bake until a toothpick inserted comes out clean (15 to 20 minutes).

# PUMPKIN MUFFINS

MAKES 12 MUFFINS

1¾ cups flour
1 teaspoon baking powder
½ teaspoon baking soda
1½ cups sugar, plus sugar for sprinkling
½ teaspoon salt
½ teaspoon ground cloves
½ teaspoon ground nutmeg

1¼ teaspoons ground cinnamon
½ cup chopped walnuts
2 eggs
½ cup vegetable oil
1 cup canned pumpkin
⅓ cup water

Preheat the oven to 375°F. In a large bowl whisk together the flour, baking powder, baking soda, the 1½ cups sugar, the salt, cloves, nutmeg, and cinnamon. Stir in the nuts. In a medium bowl beat together the eggs, oil, pumpkin, and the water; stir into the flour mixture until just combined. Divide evenly among prepared muffin cups, filling each three-fourths full. Sprinkle with the sugar and bake until a toothpick inserted comes out clean (18 to 22 minutes).

# RASPBERRY MUFFINS

MAKES 9 MUFFINS

These are some of our most requested muffins. When you serve them, make raspberry butter for an outstanding accompaniment. (Make it by substituting raspberries for the strawberries in the recipe for Strawberry Butter.) The raspberry butter and Raspberry Muffins make a sublime combination. You'll never see fresh raspberries without thinking about these muffins again!

1¾ cups flour
2½ teaspoons baking powder
½ cup sugar, plus sugar for sprinkling
½ teaspoon salt

1 egg
⅓ cup oil
¾ cup milk
1 cup raspberries, fresh or frozen

Preheat the oven to 400°F. In a medium bowl combine the flour, baking powder, the ½ cup sugar, and salt. Make a well in the center. In another medium bowl combine the egg, oil, and milk; blend well, then add to the flour mixture and stir gently. Carefully fold in the berries. Divide evenly among prepared muffin cups and bake until lightly golden (18 to 20 minutes).

# *S*OUR CREAM PRUNE PECAN MUFFINS

MAKES 12 MUFFINS

These are some of the best muffins I've ever tasted. Slightly cakelike, they're enjoyed even by people who don't like prunes. I also make them with a variation: instead of the milk, I use the same amount of water and soak the chopped prunes in it for at least fifteen minutes before making the batter. I use the prune water in the batter.

2 cups flour
1¼ cups sugar
2 teaspoons baking powder
1 teaspoon baking soda
1 teaspoon salt
2 eggs
1 cup sour cream

⅓ cup butter, melted
2½ tablespoons milk
1 teaspoon freshly grated orange zest
1 teaspoon vanilla extract
1 cup finely chopped dried pitted prunes
½ cup chopped pecans

TOPPING

2 tablespoons sugar
2 tablespoons chopped pecans

¼ teaspoon ground cinnamon

Preheat the oven to 400°F. Prepare the Topping and set aside.

In a large bowl combine the flour, sugar, baking powder, baking soda, and salt; whisk together four or five times to work air into the mixture. Make a well in the center of the mixture. In a medium bowl combine the eggs, sour cream, butter, milk, zest, and vanilla; pour into the well in the flour mixture and stir gently, then fold in the prunes and pecans.

Spoon the batter evenly among prepared muffin cups and sprinkle each muffin with the Topping. Bake until the muffins are slightly golden and spring back when touched lightly (about 20 minutes).

*Topping:* Combine the sugar, pecans, and cinnamon; mix well.

# STRAWBERRIES 'N' CREAM MUFFINS WITH STRAWBERRY BUTTER

MAKES 24 MUFFINS

2 cups sliced strawberries
2½ cups granulated sugar
3 cups flour
2 teaspoons ground cinnamon
1 teaspoon salt
1 teaspoon baking soda

2 teaspoons vanilla extract
1 cup oil or melted butter
½ cup milk
½ cup sour cream
3 eggs, beaten
1¼ cups chopped pecans

STRAWBERRY BUTTER

1 cup butter or margarine, softened
4 ounces cream cheese, at room
    temperature

⅓ cup confectioners' sugar
¼ cup mashed strawberries
Sliced fresh strawberry, for garnish

Place the strawberries in a medium bowl and sprinkle with ½ cup of the granulated sugar; set aside. Preheat the oven to 375°F.

In a large bowl combine the flour, the remaining 2 cups sugar, the cinnamon, salt, and baking soda; mix well. In a medium bowl stir together the vanilla, oil, milk, sour cream, and eggs. Add to the flour mixture and stir until just combined. Gently fold in the reserved sweetened berries and the pecans. Divide evenly among prepared muffin cups and bake until lightly golden (18 to 20 minutes). Serve with the Strawberry Butter.

*Strawberry Butter:* In the container of a blender, whip together the butter, cream cheese, and confectioners' sugar until light and fluffy. Gently fold in the mashed berries. Transfer to a serving dish and garnish with the sliced strawberry. Chill.

# $\mathscr{S}$UNSHINE ORANGE CINNAMON ROLLS

## SERVES 6 TO 8

4 tablespoons active dry yeast
1 cup warm water (105 to 115°F)
½ cup granulated sugar
½ cup orange juice, at room temperature
¼ cup vegetable oil or solid shortening,
   melted

1 egg, at room temperature
1 teaspoon salt
4 cups flour, or more as needed
1 cup butter, melted

### FILLING

½ cup granulated sugar
½ cup packed brown sugar
1 teaspoon freshly grated nutmeg

1 tablespoon ground cinnamon
2 tablespoons freshly grated orange zest

Crumble the yeast into a large bowl. Stir in the water and let stand until foamy (about 10 minutes). Add the granulated sugar and orange juice. Stir in the oil, egg, and salt. Add the flour, ½ cup at a time, stirring until the dough is smooth and elastic.

Place the dough in a large greased bowl; turn to coat the dough's entire surface. Cover and let rise in a warm, draft-free place until doubled in bulk (at least 1 hour). Meanwhile, prepare the Filling and set aside.

Generously grease a 13- by 9-inch or larger pan. Roll out the dough on a floured surface to a thickness of ¼ inch. With a pastry brush thickly coat the dough with the melted butter, then sprinkle evenly with the Filling. Roll the dough into a cylinder, as you would a jelly roll. With a string, cut the cylinder into 1-inch-thick slices. Arrange the slices in the prepared pan. Cover with a light towel and let rise in a warm place for 35 minutes.

Preheat the oven to 400°F. Bake the rolls until lightly browned on top (13 to 15 minutes).

*Filling:* In a medium bowl combine all the ingredients; mix well.

# LINNY'S SWEDISH KRINGLE

### SERVES 4 TO 6

I cook this as a breakfast treat, but I first enjoyed it as a dessert. My wonderful friend Linny made this for Dale and me one winter night when we went to visit. We played in the snow and sledded down their hill by moonlight. When it got too cold, we ran up to their beautiful log home. Linny whipped this up in no time and served it with hot chocolate. It was a fabulous way to warm up. I liked it so much, I served it everyday to our guests for a week!

The nice thing about Swedish kringle is that it appears to have taken hours to make, and you get lots of "ooh's and ah's" when you serve it. It tastes like an almond-flavored cream puff. It's a striking alternative to muffins, and easier to make than yeast-dough pastries.

8 tablespoons butter
1 cup water
1 cup flour

1 teaspoon almond extract
3 eggs

FROSTING

1 cup confectioners' sugar
1 tablespoon butter

½ teaspoon almond extract
Cream, to adjust consistency

In a medium saucepan over medium heat, combine the butter and water. Bring to a boil. Add the flour and stir until the flour doesn't stick to the sides and the mixture slips around the pan when you stir. Remove from the heat and let cool until lukewarm.

Blend in the almond extract. Add the eggs, one at a time, stirring after each addition. (The dough will be shiny and very sticky.)

Preheat the oven to 400°F. Cover a baking sheet with aluminum foil and grease it thoroughly. Place the dough on the pan and shape it either into two long logs or one large ring. Bake until golden brown and puffy (about 30 minutes). Frost while still warm.

*Frosting:* Combine all the ingredients and mix well.

# FRESH LIME SCONES WITH LIME BUTTER

### MAKES 18 SCONES

When making flavored butters, such as Julie's Lime Butter, I prefer margarine to butter. Margarine stays softer after it's whipped, whereas butter tends to harden.

4 cups flour, plus more for work surface
2 tablespoons baking powder
¼ cup sugar, plus more for sprinkling
¼ teaspoon salt
Juice and freshly grated zest of 2 large limes

8 tablespoons butter, cut into small pieces
2 eggs, beaten, at room temperature
⅔ cup buttermilk, or as needed
⅓ cup heavy cream or half-and-half

### JULIE'S LIME BUTTER

1 cup butter or margarine
4 ounces cream cheese, at room temperature

Juice and freshly grated zest of 1 lime
⅓ cup confectioners' sugar

Preheat the oven to 425°F. Grease and flour 2 baking sheets or line them with parchment paper; set aside.

Sift together the flour and baking powder 3 times, then add the ¼ cup sugar and the salt and sift again into a large bowl. Stir in the zest. Cut in the butter until the mixture is crumbly and the texture of dry oatmeal. Add the eggs, lime juice, and just enough buttermilk to form a soft, sticky dough.

Turn the dough onto a lightly floured work surface. Carefully roll or pat the dough to about ½ inch thickness, flouring when

needed to prevent sticking. Divide the dough into 3 small circles; cut each circle into 6 wedges. Place the wedges at least ¼ inch apart on the prepared baking sheets. Brush with the cream and sprinkle with the sugar. Let stand for 10 minutes, then bake until the scones are lightly golden brown (8 to 10 minutes). Serve with Julie's Lime Butter.

*Julie's Lime Butter:* In the work bowl of a food processor, or with a hand mixer, combine all the ingredients. Chill before serving.

# INDEX